LORD JIM

When Jim leaves England to begin his life as a sailor, he dreams happily of the adventures waiting for him at sea. He sees himself as the brave man who always does his duty, just like the heroes in the sea stories he read as a boy. When danger comes, he will be ready for it.

But danger does come, and Jim is not ready for it. He is the first mate on board the *Patna*, an old ship taking 800 passengers across the Indian Ocean. When the accident happens and it is time for a brave man to do his duty, Jim fails to act like the hero of his dreams. Soon, the word 'coward' is whispered around all the sea ports of the eastern seas.

Only one man believes in Jim. Marlow tries to help him find a new life, and in later years he tells the story to his friends. It is the story of Jim's search for his lost honour – a journey into the dark places of the soul, where dreams and fears move like shadows across the face of the moon . . .

OXFORD BOOKWORMS LIBRARY
Classics

Lord Jim

Stage 4 (1400 headwords)

Series Editor: Jennifer Bassett
Founder Editor: Tricia Hedge
Activities Editors: Jennifer Bassett and Alison Baxter

JOSEPH CONRAD

Lord Jim

Retold by
Clare West

OXFORD UNIVERSITY PRESS

OXFORD
UNIVERSITY PRESS

Great Clarendon Street, Oxford OX2 6DP

Oxford University Press is a department of the University of Oxford.
It furthers the University's objective of excellence in research, scholarship,
and education by publishing worldwide in

Oxford New York

Auckland Cape Town Dar es Salaam Hong Kong Karachi
Kuala Lumpur Madrid Melbourne Mexico City Nairobi
New Delhi Shanghai Taipei Toronto

With offices in

Argentina Austria Brazil Chile Czech Republic France Greece
Guatemala Hungary Italy Japan Poland Portugal Singapore
South Korea Switzerland Thailand Turkey Ukraine Vietnam

OXFORD and OXFORD ENGLISH are registered trade marks of
Oxford University Press in the UK and in certain other countries

ISBN 978 0 19 479176 2

Printed in China

ACKNOWLEDGEMENTS
Illustrated by: Ron Tiner

Word count (main text): 19,160 words

For more information on the Oxford Bookworms Library,
visit www.oup.com/bookworms

CONTENTS

STORY INTRODUCTION   i

1 Jim's early life   1
2 Marlow meets Jim   9
3 Jim tells his story   18
4 Marlow offers to help   27
5 Jim goes to Patusan   37
6 Marlow visits Jim   48
7 Jim in love, and in danger   62
8 The end of the story   74

GLOSSARY   87
ACTIVITIES: Before Reading   90
ACTIVITIES: While Reading   91
ACTIVITIES: After Reading   94
ABOUT THE AUTHOR   100
ABOUT THE BOOKWORMS LIBRARY   101

1

Jim's early life

In the Eastern ports where he worked for most of his life, Jim was very popular. He was an excellent seaman, who was liked and trusted by everyone. He was tall and strongly built, with a deep voice and a confident way of talking. To his employers and the ship captains, he was just Jim, nothing more. He had a special reason for not wanting people to know his other name. But nothing remains secret for long in sea ports, and soon someone who knew about his past was certain to arrive. When this happened, Jim always left his well-paid job immediately, and moved on to another port. Over several years he was known first in Bombay, then Calcutta, then Rangoon, Penang and Jakarta, as he moved towards the rising sun. Finally, when he could no longer bear this kind of life, he ran away from sea ports and white men for ever, hiding himself in the jungle, in a distant Malaysian village, far away from anyone who knew him. The natives of the village gave him an extra name. They called him Tuan Jim, or, as we would say, Lord Jim.

Jim had spent his childhood in a comfortable, peaceful home in the southwest of England. His father was a vicar, a kind man who always did his duty, and who had no doubts about what was right or wrong. The family house was warm and welcoming, with plenty of room for Jim and his four older brothers to play in. Close to it, on a hill, was the small grey church, standing, like a rock, where it had stood for centuries. There had been vicars in Jim's family for a hundred years, but one of his brothers had already shown an interest in the Church, so his father had to find some other work for his youngest son. When Jim spent a whole summer reading sea stories, his father was delighted, and decided that Jim would join the merchant navy at once.

He was sent to a training ship on a busy, wide river near London; there two hundred boys slept, ate and worked together, learning everything a sailor needs to know. Because he was strong, and quick, and intelligent, he learnt fast, and was generally liked. The work seemed easy to him, and he was confident of his bravery in any danger. Sometimes at night he used to forget the crowd of noisy boys around him, and escape into his own dream world of sea stories. He saw himself swimming bravely through the waves to save passengers from sinking ships, fighting natives on lonely islands, and giving orders to frightened sailors to save their lives. He was always the brave man who did his duty, just like the heroes in the stories that he had read at home.

One evening he heard a sudden shout, 'Something's happened! On deck, all of you! Hurry!' He jumped to his feet, and joined the other boys as they ran up on to the deck.

It was a dark and stormy night. The wind was blowing strongly and heavy rain was falling. Jim stood without moving, staring at the cruel black waves. Was it him that the storm wanted? What would it be like, to fall into that cold water and drown?

'Send the lifeboat out!' came the order. In the darkness two small ships had crashed into each other, and there were distant voices crying for help. Boys ran past Jim, who still did not move. They jumped into the lifeboat and began to row as fast as they could towards the two damaged ships.

'Row together, you young dogs!' shouted a voice from the boat, 'if you want to save any lives!'

Jim had now run to the side of the ship and was looking down. He felt a hand on his shoulder. 'Too late, young man,' said the captain. Jim looked up, disappointed. The captain smiled. 'Better luck next time,' he said. 'This will teach you to move quickly in an emergency.'

The lifeboat came dancing back through the waves, half full of water. The boys had saved two men, who now lay exhausted in the bottom of the boat. Jim no longer felt afraid of the sea. It seemed to him that he cared nothing for the storm. He would live through greater dangers than that, and would show the world how brave he was. That night he sat alone, while the boys who had saved the two men's lives told their excited friends the whole story. When they described the waves, and the cold, and the sinking ships, Jim felt angry. They were so proud of what they had done! He, too, had wanted to show his bravery. But

3

'*Too late, young man,*' *said the captain.*

perhaps it was better this way. He had learnt more from this experience than any of them. The next time a brave man was needed, he alone, he felt sure, would know how to fight the wind and the seas. And as the other boys talked and laughed together, Jim dreamed happily of the next adventure and his chance to prove himself.

After two years of training, he went to sea. He made many voyages on many different ships, but surprisingly there were no adventures. The sea had not yet tested him, or shown him the secret truth of his pretences. However, although he was still very young, he soon became chief mate of a fine ship. Unfortunately, he was badly hurt during a storm at sea, and when the ship reached an Eastern port, he was taken to hospital. His broken leg needed time to mend, and so he was left behind when his ship sailed away.

Time passed slowly in the hospital, where the patients played cards, and slept, and told each other stories. There were brightly coloured flowers in the gardens, and warm, soft air blew in through the open windows. The hospital was on a hill, and had an excellent view of the port, which was always busy, as it was on one of the main sea routes to the East. Jim felt wonderfully calm as he looked out every day at the ships like toys in the sea, with the endless blue of the Eastern sky above, and the smiling peace of the Eastern seas all around.

As soon as he could walk, he left the hospital and started looking for a ship to take him back to England. While waiting, he naturally spent time with other European seamen in the port. Many of them had become lazy. They were used to the easy life of a white sailor in the East, and did not want to return to the bad weather, harder conditions and more dangerous duties of the West. They talked, not of work, but of luck, and chance, and money. At first, Jim refused to listen to them. But soon he began to find these men strangely interesting. How did they make a success of their lives, with so little work and so little danger? And suddenly, he decided not to go home to England, and took a job as chief mate of the *Patna*.

The *Patna* was a local ship, as old as the hills, and in very bad condition. Her captain was a German whose home was in Australia, a very large, fat, cruel man, who felt that he owed no duty to anybody. He had arranged to take eight hundred pilgrims to the city of Mecca in Saudi Arabia.

Jim watched as the native people hurried on to the ship, filling every corner like water in a container. Eight hundred men and women had come from north and south, from islands and villages, over mountains and down rivers. At the call of an idea they had left their forests, their farms, their homes - strong men, young boys, little girls, women with heads covered, and sleeping babies. 'Look at these animals,' said the German captain to his new chief mate.

The *Patna* left the port, and started across the Indian Ocean towards the Red Sea. The five white seamen lived separately from the pilgrims, who were packed close together on every deck and in every corner. The days were hot and heavy, and the ship moved slowly across a flat, lifeless sea. There were no clouds in the burning sky, and it was too hot to think or feel.

The nights were beautiful. A wonderful calm seemed to cover the world, and the young moon shone down on the smooth, cool sea. Jim thought that there was nothing but peace and happiness in nature, as he breathed in the soft air, while in all the dark corners around him the pilgrims slept, trusting the white men to keep them safe.

Two Malays stood silently at the wheel. Jim walked along the deck, and looked at the dark water. He did not see the shadow of what was to come. In fact, he felt that nothing could hurt him on a night like this. He had been responsible for the ship for several hours now, and he was feeling sleepy.

'Anything to report?' The captain had come up noiselessly behind him. His face was red, with one eye half closed, the other staring and glassy. His fat body shook when he walked, and his clothes were dirty and unbuttoned. Jim answered his captain politely, but moved a little away from the ugly figure who had destroyed the night's peace.

The ship continued to move smoothly over the flat sea. 'You can't imagine how hot it is down below,' said a voice. It was the young second engineer, who had come up on deck for some fresh air. He did not seem able to speak clearly. 'Why I work on this old ship, I don't know,' he went on. 'We engineers work twice as hard as you sailors, and—'

'Don't speak to me like that, you dog!' shouted the

captain. 'Where did you get your drink?'

'Not from you, captain!' laughed the engineer. 'You're too mean for that! No, the good old chief gave me some.'

The chief engineer was a well-known drinker, who normally kept his drink to himself. Tonight, however, he had given some to the second engineer, who was not used to it. The chief and the captain had worked together on many ships, and people in the *Patna*'s home port said that they had been guilty of every crime you could think of, at one time or another.

Jim watched the captain getting angrier and angrier, and the young man shouting louder and louder. He smiled to himself. These men did not belong to the world of adventure. They had nothing to do with him. He was almost asleep on his feet.

Suddenly the engineer was thrown forward on to his face, and lay silent on the deck. Jim and the captain stared at the calm sea, and looked up at the stars. What had happened? They could still hear the engines turning. Had the earth stopped? Now the cloudless sky and the quiet sea looked less safe than before. 'What was that?' cried the engineer, holding his arm in pain. There was a noise like distant thunder, and the ship trembled. The two Malays at the wheel looked at the white men, but received no orders, so did not move. The *Patna* lifted a little in the water, and then continued smoothly on her way.

2

Marlow meets Jim

A month or so later, at the official inquiry, Jim was asked what had happened to the *Patna*. Trying to describe the experience honestly, he replied, 'The ship went over whatever it was as easily as oil running over a stick.'

The inquiry was held in the crowded police court of an Eastern port. Jim stood there, in front of them all, while many eyes looked at him out of dark, white, and red faces, like staring shadows. They saw a large, good-looking young man, with a straight back and unhappy eyes. The three judges, two of whom were sea captains, sat together under a large window. They asked Jim clear questions, which he answered truthfully. Outside, the sun was beating down, and the air was heavy in the courtroom. Jim's voice seemed very loud to him; it was the only sound in the world. The painful questions they asked him appeared to come from inside him, like the questioning of his conscience.

'So after you realized the ship had hit something underwater, your captain ordered you to go and see if there was any damage?' asked one of the sea captains.

'Yes,' said Jim. 'I discovered a big hole in the metal wall of the ship, below the water. I didn't think of danger just

9

then. I was surprised, because it had happened so quickly. I was on my way back to tell the captain, when I met the second engineer. He had broken his left arm when he was thrown forward earlier. When I told him about the damage, he cried, "My God! The whole ship will be full of water in a minute!" He pushed me away with his right arm and ran up on to the bridge, shouting as he went. I followed him, and was in time to see the captain hit him. The captain ordered him to keep quiet and go and stop the engines.'

Jim hoped that if he described everything exactly, and gave all the facts, the people in the courtroom would understand the full horror of it. Every small detail of what had happened was important. Fortunately he remembered it all very clearly. There was something else as well, something unseen and evil, that had helped to cause the disaster. He wished to make that clear. He wanted to go on talking, to find out the truth. But although he spoke calmly and carefully, he felt like a trapped animal, desperately searching for a way out.

The questioning continued. Jim was beginning to feel very tired. His mouth was tastelessly dry, and his head felt hot, while the rest of his body was cold. While he waited for the next question, his eyes rested on a white man sitting by himself. He had a worn, clouded face, with clear, quiet eyes. Jim answered another question, and wanted to cry out, 'Is it worth going on? Is it really worth it?' He met the eyes of the white man, who was looking at him differently from all the others in the courtroom. It was an honest, intelligent look. Telling the truth was not enough, thought Jim; words were no good to him any longer. And that man appeared to understand his hopeless difficulty.

That stranger with the clear, quiet eyes was Marlow. And later on, in distant parts of the world, Marlow often remembered Jim, and talked about him. It was usually after dinner in a friend's house, when men sat comfortably in their armchairs on the veranda and smoked their cigars, that Marlow was asked to talk. In the darkness, as he sat surrounded by sweet-smelling flowers and a group of listening men, every detail of that fresh young face and straight figure came back to Marlow. He could almost imagine himself back in the past, and he often began with a warning to his listeners.

------------------------------- ✳ -------------------------------

My friends, it's easy enough to talk about young Jim, but don't be too quick to judge him. A good dinner, an excellent cigar, and a beautiful evening of freshness and starlight like this make us forget how difficult life can be. We all try to do what is right, but the best of us can take the wrong route occasionally. Yes, I was at the official inquiry, and saw Jim there, but I had seen him before.

The first news we had of the *Patna* was a mysterious message from Aden, that a damaged ship full of pilgrims had been found without its officers, in the Indian Ocean. The whole waterfront – boatmen, natives, officials, clerks – talked of nothing else for two weeks. Then, one fine morning, I was standing near the port office, when I saw four men walking towards me, and suddenly realized that they must be the missing officers from the *Patna*. I recognized the captain, a fat, ugly German, who was well known in all the Eastern ports as an irresponsible and dishonest seaman. Behind him was the chief engineer, a tall, thin man, and the second engineer, with a broken arm. The fourth was a young man with fair hair and square shoulders, who stood with his hands in his pockets, turning his back on the others. This was my first view of Jim, and I was strangely interested in him, because he looked so clean-faced, so strong, so brave. I felt almost angry. If a man who looks like that can go wrong, I thought, who can you trust?

Captain Elliott was the chief port official in those days, and as soon as he realized the captain of the *Patna* had arrived, he sent for him. Elliott believed strongly in duty and responsibility, and didn't mind who he shouted at. Through the open windows of his office we all heard what he thought of the *Patna*'s captain, and in a very few moments the fat man came running angrily out of Elliott's office. He saw me looking at him, and said, 'That crazy Englishman in there called me a dog!' I smiled. 'Dog' was the politest word that had reached me. 'But I don't care!' he continued, his face purple with anger. 'The Pacific is big, my friend. If you English take away my master's certificate, if you won't let me command a ship here, I'll go to – to Apia, to Honolulu – they know me there!' I could easily imagine what kind of people knew him there.

I looked over at the young man again, wanting to see him

This was my first view of Jim.

angry, unhappy, ashamed. But he looked completely unworried, and I couldn't understand it. I liked the look of him; he appeared to be that good, honest kind of man who is not interested in ideas, but who does his work well and lives his life bravely to the end. I've had my own ship for a long time now, and I've trained enough young sailors in my time to be able to judge whether you can trust a man or not. It worried me that perhaps I had made a mistake with Jim. Was there something missing in his character? What had made him act like that?

The two engineers were now standing in front of their captain, but he turned away from them and hurried over to a horse and trap. He climbed in, shouted impatiently at the driver, and before anyone could do anything to stop him, the horse and trap disappeared in a cloud of dust. Where did he go? To Apia, or Honolulu? Nobody ever saw him again.

At the official inquiry, which took place a week later, and lasted three days, Jim was the only one who was questioned. The captain had escaped, and both the engineers were in hospital. The one with the broken arm had a bad fever, and the chief engineer had been drinking brandy for three days and could no longer talk sensibly. In my opinion, the only truth worth knowing was not how, but why, the officers had left the ship, and I realized the inquiry would not discover this. Judges are not paid to look into a man's soul, but only to see the results of his actions.

One of the inquiry officials was Captain Brierly, known in all the Eastern ports as a brave officer and an excellent seaman. Young, healthy and successful, he seemed to be one of those lucky men who never make a mistake, and who therefore have a high opinion of themselves. We all thought nothing could touch him or his self-confidence. But we were wrong, because he killed himself a week after the inquiry. I think now that while the other two judges were questioning Jim, Brierly was holding his own silent inquiry, questioning himself. I think his conscience was accusing him of – who knows what? It wasn't anything to do with money, or drink, or women. But at the end of it, he found himself guilty, and drowned himself, leaving letters for his chief mate and the ship's owners.

During the inquiry I had a conversation with him, which I remember especially well, because of his sudden death only a few days later. He spoke to me at the end of the first day.

'Don't you think it's stupid?' he asked me angrily. I looked at him in surprise. Brierly was normally very calm. 'Why are we attacking that young man? Why should he eat all that dirt? Why doesn't he run away?'

'He probably hasn't any money,' I answered.

'We should put an end to this now,' Brierly continued. 'This kind of thing destroys people's confidence in us seamen. I'll give you some money, Marlow, and you talk to him. Tell him to leave. Give him another chance. People will forget about it very soon, and he can get on with his life. Of course I can't suggest this to him myself, but *you* could.'

And so I saw, just for a moment, the real Brierly. Naturally I refused to do what he wanted, because I didn't like the way he expected *me* to arrange Jim's escape, and because I thought it was brave of Jim to accept the blame. I certainly did not realize how important it was to Brierly, who was perhaps remembering some mistake in his own past.

At the end of the second day of the inquiry, I was talking to someone I knew, while leaving the courtroom. I noticed Jim's wide shoulders in front of us. My friend saw a yellow dog running between people's legs, and said with a laugh, 'Look at that miserable dog!' I saw Jim turn round immediately. He stepped forward and stared at me. My friend reached the door and went out, and the crowd disappeared. Suddenly Jim and I were alone, where there had been hundreds of people a few moments earlier. The building was strangely silent.

'Did you speak to me?' asked Jim, very low. His face was darkening, and he looked violent.

'No,' I said, watching him. 'You've made a mistake.'

'I won't let anyone call me names outside this court,' he said. I could see that he was deeply angry, although he spoke so quietly.

'But I really don't know what you mean,' I said, trying hard to remember what I had said or done.

'I'll soon show you I'm not a dog!' he cried, moving towards me.

Then, finally, I understood. 'My God!' I said. 'You don't think I called you a . . .'

'But I'm sure . . . I heard someone say it,' he replied.

Silently I showed him the corner of the building, where

the dog was sitting in the shadows. At first he did not seem to understand, then he looked surprised, and then ashamed. The red of his fair, sunburnt skin deepened suddenly from his neck right up to his hair. I felt very sorry for him. He had opened his soul to me, and got nothing back. He turned and ran outside.

I had to run fast to catch up with him, and started a breathless conversation. By now his self-control had returned, and he apologized. 'You see,' he explained, 'there are so many staring people in court who probably think – what I thought you said. In court I have to accept that, and I do, but outside it's different.'

I don't pretend I understood him, but I wanted to know more about him, so I invited him to dinner at the Malabar House Hotel, where I was staying.

3

Jim tells his story

The big hotel dining-room was more than half full of people, eating, drinking and talking, while the dark-faced waiters hurried from table to table. And opposite me sat Jim, with his blue, boyish eyes looking straight into mine. I liked his young, honest face and his seriousness. He was the right kind; he was one of us. But how could he talk so calmly? Was it because he was controlling himself, or because he did not care?

Towards the end of dinner, I mentioned the inquiry. 'It must be awfully hard for you,' I said.

I was surprised by what happened next. He put out a hand quickly and held my arm, staring fixedly at me. 'It is – hell,' he cried. People at tables near us turned to look. I stood up, and we went outside, to sit on the veranda with our coffee and cigars. From our chairs we looked out at the sea, where the lights of the ships shone like stars in the thick, warm darkness.

'I couldn't run away,' Jim began. 'The captain did, but that's no good for me. The others have got out of it too, but I couldn't, and I wouldn't. I can never go home now, you know. I'm sure my dear old Dad has seen the story in the newspapers by now. I can never explain all this to the poor old man. He wouldn't understand.'

I looked up. I had the feeling he was extremely fond of his 'old Dad', and I imagined how proud the country vicar had been of his sailor son.

Jim went on, 'Look, you mustn't think I'm like those others – you know, the captain and the engineers. What happened to me was different.' I said nothing to agree or disagree with this, but I didn't know if he really believed what he was saying. 'I don't know what I'll do after the inquiry. Nobody will employ me as an officer again. I haven't any money to go anywhere else. I'll have to get occasional work on a ship, as an ordinary seaman.'

'Do you think you can?' I asked. I wanted to hurt him, to break his self-control.

He jumped up and turned away, then came back and looked miserably down at me. 'Why did you say that? You've been very kind to me. You didn't laugh when I—' here his voice trembled '—made that stupid mistake.' Looking away from me, he stared into the darkness. 'It's a question of being ready. I wasn't, not then.' And then, turning to me, 'Look, I'd like to explain – I'd like somebody to understand – one person at least! You! Why not you? Ah! What a chance I missed! My God! What a chance I missed!'

He was silent for a while, with a quiet, distant look in his eyes, as he thought of that lost opportunity. I watched him moving into his own private world of heroic dreams and adventures. Ah, he was romantic! He was very far away from me, although his chair was only a metre away from mine. Suddenly I saw from his delighted expression that he had reached the heart of his impossible world, and come to the end of his perfect dream. His young face wore a smile that your faces will never wear, my friends, nor mine either.

I brought him roughly back to the present by saying, 'You missed a chance when you left the ship, you mean!'

He turned quickly towards me, his dream broken and his eyes suddenly full of pain. 'You see,' he said after a moment, 'the hole in the side of the ship was so big! A piece of metal as big as my hand fell off while I was looking at it!'

'That made you feel bad,' I said.

'Do you suppose I was thinking of myself? There were eight hundred people on that ship, and only seven boats. I expected to see the hole widen and the water flow over them as they lay sleeping . . . What could I do?' He passed a hand over his head. 'The captain had sent me to check the damage again. At first I wanted to wake all the passengers up, but my mouth was too dry, and I couldn't speak. I felt completely helpless. When I looked at the unconscious sleepers around me, I saw dead men. Nothing could save them! There was no time! I could not repair the damage, and I could not save eight hundred people in seven boats! I saw, as clearly as I see you now, that there was nothing I could do. It seemed to take all the life out of my body. I just stood there and waited. Do you think I am afraid of death?' He banged his hand angrily on the table, so that the coffee cups danced. 'My God! I tell you I am not!'

'*I saw that there was nothing I could do.*'

He was not afraid of death, perhaps, but, my friends, I'll tell you what he was afraid of – the emergency. He was able to imagine, only too well, all the horrors of the end – water filling the ship, people screaming, boats sinking – all the terrible details of a disaster at sea. I think he was ready to die, but I suspect he wanted to die quietly, peacefully. Not many men are prepared to continue their fight to the end, when they find themselves losing to a much stronger enemy, like the sea.

'The engines had stopped, and it seemed very quiet on the ship,' he went on. 'I ran back up to the bridge, and found the captain and the two engineers trying to lower one of the ship's boats down into the sea. "Quick!" the captain whispered to me. "Help us, man!"

'"Aren't you going to do something?" I asked.

'"Yes! I'm going to get away," he said over his shoulder.

'I didn't understand then what he meant. The three of them were desperately pulling and pushing at the boat, and calling each other names, but something was wrong with the ropes and the boat wouldn't move. I stood away from them, watching the sea, black and calm and deadly. My head was full of ideas, and I was thinking hard, but I couldn't see any chance of survival for us. You think I'm a coward, because I just stood there, but what would *you* do? You can't tell – nobody can. I needed time . . .'

He was breathing quickly. He was not speaking to me, but seemed to be on trial in front of an unseen judge, who was responsible for his soul. This was a matter too difficult for the court of inquiry to decide. It was about the true nature of life, about light and darkness, truth and lies, good and evil.

As he spoke, his eyes shone. 'Ever since I was a boy, I've been preparing myself for difficulties and danger. I was ready, I tell you! Ready for anything! But—' and the light went out of his face '—this was so unexpected! Well, I'll tell you the rest. As I was standing there on the bridge, the second engineer ran up and begged me to help them. I pushed him away, in fact I hit him. "Won't you save your own life – you coward?" he cried. Coward! That's what he called me. Ha! ha! ha!'

Jim threw himself back in his chair and laughed loudly. I had never heard anything as bitter as that noise. All around us on the veranda conversation stopped. People stared at him.

After a while he continued with his story. 'I was saying to the *Patna*, "Sink! Go on, sink!" I wanted it to finish. Then in the sky I saw a big black thunder cloud coming towards us, and I knew the ship couldn't survive a storm. I saw that George, the third engineer, had now joined the other three, who were still trying to get the boat lowered. Suddenly George fell backwards, and lay without moving on the deck. He was dead. Heart trouble, I think. And just then there was a loud crash as the captain and the two others managed to get the boat down into the water. They were in the boat, and I could hear them shouting from below, "Jump, George! Jump!"'

Jim trembled a little, and then sat very still, as he relived the awful moment. 'There were eight hundred living people on that ship, and they were shouting for the one dead man to jump! "Jump, George, we'll catch you!" I felt the ship move

'They were shouting for the one dead man to jump.'

– I thought she was going down, under me . . .' Jim put his hand to his head again, and paused for a moment. 'I had jumped . . . it seems,' he added. His clear blue eyes looked miserably at me, and I felt like an old man helplessly watching a childish disaster.

'It seems you did,' I agreed.

'When I was in the boat, I wished I could die. But I couldn't go back. I'd jumped into an everlasting deep hole . . .'

Nothing could be more true. He described to me the full horror of the hours he spent in that small boat with the three men. They called him evil names, angrily accused him of killing George, even talked of throwing him out of the boat. 'I didn't care what happened to me,' Jim went on. 'I wondered if I would go crazy, or kill myself. You see, I had saved my own life, while everything that was important to me had sunk with the ship in the night. We were certain the ship had sunk, you know. As we rowed away, we couldn't hear any cries, or see her lights. The captain said we were lucky to survive. And I decided not to kill myself. The right thing was to go on, wait for another chance, test myself . . .' After a long silence, he continued, 'Another ship picked us up the next day. The captain and the others pretended we had tried to save the passengers, but the *Patna* had sunk too fast. The story didn't matter to me. I had jumped, hadn't I? That's what I had to live with. It was like cheating the dead.'

'And there were no dead,' I said.

He turned away from me at that. I knew that a French ship had found the *Patna* sailing out of control. The captain had put several of his officers on board, and they sailed her to the nearest port, Aden. Although the *Patna* was badly damaged, it had not sunk, and nobody had died, except George, the third engineer, whose body was found on the bridge. The pilgrims were all put on to other ships to continue their journey to Mecca.

But everybody went on talking about the *Patna*. And now, when seamen meet in the Eastern ports, they very often discuss the strange story of the pilgrim ship, and the officers who ran away, just as I am telling you about it tonight.

4

Marlow offers to help

Our coffee and cigars were finished. I knew that tomorrow – or was it today? It was well past midnight – the inquiry judges would take up the weapon of the law and punish Jim. I told myself repeatedly that the young man was guilty, but I wanted to help him get away. My friends, if you can't understand my reasons, you haven't been listening to me all this time.

So I suggested Brierly's plan of escape to Jim. I would lend him some money – he could pay it back when he liked – and I would also write a letter to a friend of mine in Rangoon, who would give him a job. Jim could leave that same day, and save himself the shame of the final day in the crowded courthouse. I was impatient to begin writing the letter immediately. But Jim refused.

'Run away? No, I couldn't think of it,' he said, shaking his head. 'It's awfully good of you, but no.'

I am sure that things looked terribly uncertain to him at that moment, but he did not hesitate. He was young and strong, and there was something fine in his wild hope that he would survive.

I felt angry, however. 'The whole miserable business is bitter enough for a man like you . . .' I started saying.

'Yes, it is, it is,' he whispered, his eyes fixed on the floor. The way he spoke touched me to the heart. 'The captain escaped – the others went to hospital – they all got away . . .' He waved them scornfully away with his hand. 'But I've got to accept this thing. I'm not going to avoid any of it.'

'Oh really, my dear man . . .' I said crossly.

'You don't understand,' he replied, looking straight into my eyes. 'I jumped, but I don't run away.'

Neither of us knew how to continue the conversation. I stood up at last, saying, 'I had no idea it was so late.'

'I expect you've had enough of this,' he said, 'and to tell you the truth, so have I.'

Well, he had refused my offer of help, and he was ready to go now. Outside, the night was waiting for him, quietly and dangerously. For a few seconds we stood together silently.

'What will you do after – after . . .?' I asked, very low.

'Go to hell, probably,' he replied.

I judged it best to answer lightly, 'Please remember, I would very much like to see you before you go.'

'Nothing will prevent you,' he said bitterly. 'Everybody will know where I am.'

And then, as we said goodbye, he stupidly imagined that I did not want to shake hands with him. First he offered his hand, then pulled back, then hesitated, then – it was too awful for words. I had to shout at him, 'Jim! Shake hands with me, man!' Finally it was over, and he disappeared into the night. I heard his heavy footsteps. He was running, with nowhere to go to. And he was only twenty-three.

Next morning, the last day of the inquiry, I was in court again. It was really very wrong of me, because my chief mate was expecting me to visit my ship, but I had to know what would happen to Jim. Outside, the streets were full of colour and bright sunshine, but the courtroom was dark and airless. Jim stood there, pink and fair and serious, while the judge spoke. 'This court has decided that the officers of the *Patna*, who were responsible for all the ship's passengers, were guilty of forgetting their clear duty, when they left the ship in the moment of danger. The court has therefore decided to take away the master's certificates of the captain and chief mate.'

The room was silent, then people started to leave. I saw Jim, his face as black as thunder, walking out slowly and a little uncertainly. As I was watching him, a man called Chester spoke to me. I knew him a little. He was a West Australian who normally traded in the Pacific, but had come here looking for a cheap ship to buy. He watched Jim walking away.

'That young man's no good, is he?' he said. 'But I can give him a job. I've discovered a guano island among the Walpole rocks which is going to make me rich. It's rocky, and a bit dangerous to land there. I can't get anybody to take the job, but I need a man to do the work there for me. I don't care if he's a bit of a coward, or hasn't got his certificate. He'll have forty natives to collect the guano, and I'll give him a couple of guns, of course. You could persuade him to take the job, Marlow, couldn't you?'

I stared at him in horror. I knew the place he was talking about. There was no water on the island and very little rain

Jim stood there while the judge spoke.

fell there. I had a sudden picture of Jim on a shadowless rock, up to his knees in guano, with the screams of seabirds in his ears, and the sun beating down on his head.

'I wouldn't advise my worst enemy to accept your offer,' I said scornfully.

'It's just the job for him.' Chester smiled unpleasantly. 'I can promise the island wouldn't sink under him – and I believe he's a bit sensitive on that question.'

'Good morning,' I said sharply, and walked away, leaving him staring angrily after me.

I hurried down to the waterside, and found Jim looking miserably at the sea. He didn't hear me come up, but turned quickly when I touched his shoulder. He followed me back to the hotel obediently. I realized that he had nowhere in the whole world where he could be alone with his suffering.

He spent the rest of the day in my room, where he stood looking out on the veranda, while I sat at my desk, busily writing letters. We did not speak to each other. I wrote all the letters I owed people, and then I wrote to people who would certainly be surprised to receive a letter from me. It became dark, and still I went on writing. It was clear that he was very unhappy. Occasionally I saw his strong shoulders shaking, and I was glad his family could not see him like that. Suddenly, with a crash, he pushed open the glass door on to the veranda, and stepped out into the blackness, standing there like a lonely figure by a dark and hopeless sea. I began to think he was taking it all too seriously. Should I persuade him to accept Chester's offer? I knew there was nothing except myself between him and the dark sea. But I said nothing.

The time was coming when I would hear him described as a hero. It's true, I tell you. Towards the end, he found honour and a perfect happiness in the Malaysian jungle. When I saw him for the last time, a few years later, he was completely in control, strong and successful, loved and trusted by the natives of Patusan. But that is not the way I remember him. I shall always see his lonely, shaking figure on that hotel veranda, suffering in the darkness.

A crash of thunder made me lift my head, and lightning suddenly lit up the night. A few moments later, we were in the middle of a storm, with an angry wind shaking the windows. He stepped inside, closing the door behind him.

'Well, that's over,' he said, sounding almost normal. This encouraged me to look up at him. 'I think I'm all right now,' he went on. 'Thank you – for letting me – here in your room – nowhere else to go.' The rain was falling heavily on the veranda by now. 'Well – goodbye,' he said, and turned to go.

'Wait! Come back!' I cried. 'Look! Let me help you!'

'You can't,' he replied miserably. 'I can't take money . . .'

'It's not money I'm offering you!' I answered angrily. 'Look at this letter I'm writing! It's to a man I know well, asking him to give you work. I would only do this for a good friend. Just think about that.'

His face changed in a moment. 'My God!' he shouted. 'I never realized! How can I thank you? It's just what I wanted – an opportunity to start again! I know I can do it! Look – I'm sorry – I can't stay – I'm too excited!'

I waved my hand as he ran from the room. I had probably saved him from an early death, or perhaps from madness, but I felt sad. He was so young, and believed so fully in himself and in the beauty of life! I was no longer young, and I knew that his fate, like mine, was written in large letters on the face of a rock, and nothing he could do would change it.

My friend not only employed Jim, but welcomed him into his house. Unfortunately, only a year later, the second engineer from the *Patna* arrived unexpectedly in Rangoon, and Jim decided to leave the port at once. I was extremely disappointed to hear this, but helped Jim to find a second job in a port a thousand kilometres south of there. His new employers thought a lot of Jim, and trusted him with all their business. But one day the name of the *Patna* was mentioned, and Jim was too sensitive to bear it. Again, he left the place immediately. From now on, he moved from port to port to find work, trying to hide his terrible secret, until someone who knew the story spoke of it, and then he moved on again. I felt responsible for him, and helped and encouraged him as much as I could, but I knew that he was losing confidence in himself, although he was always cheerful and polite to me. What would be the end of it all? How long could Jim go on running away from his past?

I decided to ask for advice from someone I trusted more than most men. He was a rich German trader called Stein, who had a large business buying and selling all kinds of things in the islands, ports and jungle villages of the East. He was tall and thin, with a sympathetic, intelligent face, and white hair brushed back from a high forehead. Although his life had been long and adventurous, he now spent most of his time studying and collecting butterflies. In fact, by now he had become a world-famous collector. He was liked by everyone, for the bravery of his past, and the kindness he showed to all of us.

When I visited him in his large, dark study, he was looking delightedly at the best butterfly in his collection. 'A wonderful example!' he said, smiling. 'So beautiful! So perfect!'

'I have another example of nature to discuss with you,' I said. 'But I'm afraid it's a man, not an insect.'

His smile disappeared, but he listened encouragingly. 'I understand very well,' he said, when I had finished telling him Jim's story. 'He is romantic.'

I felt like a patient asking his doctor for advice, so it seemed natural to say, 'What is good for it?'

'There is only one kind of medicine! One thing alone can stop us from being ourselves – death!'

The problem appeared simple, but hopeless. 'Yes,' I said, 'so, the real question is not how to get better, but how to go on living.'

Stein agreed sadly. 'For a butterfly it is enough to be beautiful, and to live. But for man it is different, if he is sensitive. Every time he shuts his eyes, he sees himself as a hero, as a perfect man. It's all a dream – he can never be as fine as that. And so it is painful when he opens his eyes, to find he cannot make his dream come true. It is terrible for

'I have another example of nature to discuss with you.'

him. But you ask me – how to live?' His voice sounded
suddenly strong and confident. He looked away from me into
the shadows of his past. 'There is only one way. Follow the
dream, and again, follow the dream, and so – to the end.'

No doubt Stein was right. He had travelled very far in life,
always bravely, always without hesitating, and fate had
brought him friends, love, adventure. But it seemed a lonely,

difficult life to me. 'Nobody could be more romantic than you,' I told him. 'And sometimes you dream of a beautiful butterfly, but when it appears, you don't let the opportunity go, do you? You catch it! But Jim—'

Stein lifted his hand. 'Do you know how many opportunities I have missed? How many dreams I have lost?' He shook his head sadly. 'Perhaps I myself don't know. Everyone knows of one or two dreams like that. And that is the trouble . . . Well, it's getting late. Tonight you will sleep here, and tomorrow we will think of a way of helping the young man.'

He showed me to my room, and shook hands with me. 'Good night,' he said. I watched him return the way he had come. He was going back to his butterflies.

5

Jim goes to Patusan

Marlow's cigar had gone out. He stood up, moved to the edge of the veranda, and stared out into the darkness. Behind him, the circle of listeners in their armchairs waited for the story to continue. At last, one of them said encouragingly, 'Well?'

Marlow turned to face them, carefully relit his cigar, and then continued with his story.

———————— ❋ ————————

I don't suppose any of you have heard of Patusan? It doesn't matter. There are many stars in the sky that most people have never heard of, and which are of no importance to them anyway. Patusan was like one of these stars. It was occasionally mentioned by officials in Batavia, and it was known by name to a very few in the trading world. But nobody had ever been there, and, I suspect, nobody *wanted* to go there. That was where Stein arranged to send Jim. It was like sending him to the moon; he left his past world behind him, and started a completely new life.

Stein knew more about Patusan than anybody else. I have no doubt he had been there, perhaps looking for butterflies, when he was younger. It was at breakfast the next morning after our talk about Jim that he mentioned the place. I had just repeated what poor Brierly had said to me, 'He should creep away somewhere and hide.'

Stein looked up at me with interest. 'That could be done,' he said, drinking his coffee.

'You know, bury himself somewhere,' I explained.

'Yes, he is young, and could make another life for himself. Well, there is Patusan.' He added, 'And the woman is dead now.'

I didn't know the woman he had mentioned, but I learnt from Stein that she had been an intelligent, good-looking Dutch-Malay girl. She had married a worthless Portuguese man, who made her life extremely miserable. Because Stein felt sorry for her, he gave her husband a job, as manager of Stein & Company's trading-post in Patusan. Unfortunately, the Portuguese, whose name was Cornelius, was dishonest and lazy, so the trading-post lost money. Now that the woman had died, Stein wanted to replace Cornelius, and he generously suggested offering the job to Jim.

'There may be some difficulty with Cornelius,' said Stein. 'He'll be angry with Jim for taking his job. I don't think he'll want to leave Patusan, so he may cause trouble. But that has nothing to do with me. As he has a daughter, I think I shall let him keep the house he's been living in, if he wants to stay.'

Patusan is an area of deep jungle, far up the river, about sixty kilometres from the sea. There is a native village of the same name. Behind the roofs of the native houses, you can see the forest, and behind that there are two steep hills very close together, separated by a narrow valley. I saw all this later, when I visited Jim in Patusan. We were standing outside the very fine house that he had built for himself, on a warm, silent evening, watching an almost full moon rise behind the black hills. Red, and round, and nearly perfect, it sailed slowly upwards between the sides of the valley, finally moving away above the hill-tops, like a soul escaping from a buried body.

'Wonderful effect,' said Jim by my side. 'Worth seeing, isn't it?' He spoke proudly, and that made me smile. Did he feel he could control even the movements of the moon? He was in control of so many things in Patusan! Things that had once seemed as far beyond his control as the moon and the stars.

But Stein and I had no idea of this when we talked about sending him to Patusan. We both wanted to get him away, away from *himself* rather than anyone else. We knew he would be safer in a quiet, lonely place, with nobody who knew or cared about his past.

I must tell you, however, that I had another reason for sending him away. I was about to go home to England for a while, and I think I wanted, more than I myself realized at the time, to be free of him – do you understand? – before I left. I was going home, and he had come to me from there, with his miserable trouble and his shadowy dreams, like a man carrying something heavy on his tired shoulders in a thick mist. I cannot say I had ever seen him clearly, right up to the day when I had my last view of him. But the less I understood him, the closer I felt to him. After all, I did not

39

We were watching an almost full moon rise behind the black hills.

know much more about myself. And then, I repeat, I was
going home – to that distant place we all come from. We, the
famous and the unknown, travel in our thousands all over
the world, earning beyond the seas our good name, our
fortune or perhaps just enough bread for that day. But when

we go home, we meet again our friends, our family, and others
– those whom we obey and those whom we love. More than
that, we have to meet the soul of the country, that lives in its
air, in its valleys, in its rivers and its trees – a wordless friend
and judge. To breathe in the peace of home, to be happy there,
I think we have to return with a clear conscience. I know that
Jim felt something of this. He would never go home now.
Never! He could not bear the idea of it.

And so, like a much older brother, I felt responsible for
Jim. I was worried about what would happen to him. For
example, he could start drinking. The world is small, and I
was afraid of meeting him one day, in a foreign port, a red-
eyed, dirty drunk, asking to borrow five dollars from me.
You know how often that happens, when you can only just
recognize a sadly changed figure from the past, who reappears
in your life for a moment. That seemed the worst danger I
could see for him or for me, but I knew I had no imagination.
And Jim had plenty. People with imagination often go further
than others in life, for good or evil. How could I tell what
Jim would do?

You see, I'm telling you so much about my fears for him
because there is not much of the story left. I hear you ask,
was I right to be afraid for him? I won't say. Perhaps you can
decide, better than I can. Anyway, Jim did not go wrong, not
at all. In fact, he developed wonderfully, and lived his life
bravely and honestly to the end. I ought to be delighted,
because I was closely involved in his success. But somehow I
am not as pleased as I expected to be. I ask myself if he really

managed to carry himself out of that mist in which I had seen him. And another thing, the last word has not been said – will probably never be said. Our lives are too short for anyone to judge us fully. And we ourselves never have time to say our last word – the last word of our love, our trust, our sadness, our guilt, our fight against the darkness.

I won't tell you much more about Jim. In my opinion he reached greatness, but you may see it differently. My words may not be enough to persuade you, as I'm afraid you people think more of your bodies than your imaginations. I don't want to be rude; it is sensible to have no dreams – and safe – and useful – and boring. But surely, my friends, you too have known, once in your time, the brightness of life, the fire that burns in you so strongly and unexpectedly, then, too soon, disappears!

Jim's fame never reached the outside world, of course, from a place so lonely and far from anywhere. At one time Patusan was famous for its pepper, and in the seventeenth century Dutch and English traders travelled far through the jungle in their desperate search for this valuable plant. These heroic adventurers did not care about disease, hunger or death. Some of them left their bones whitening in a distant land, so that companies at home could make fortunes selling pepper. For a hundred years, they sent back news of Patusan, describing its rivers and jungle, its natives and customs, and the great Sultan who controlled the fate of all who lived there.

But now the pepper has all gone, nobody writes or talks about Patusan any longer, and the present Sultan is a young boy whose uncles have stolen his fortune.

It was Stein who told me all this. He was perfectly honest with me over the breakfast table that morning. It was an extremely dangerous place, where people could lose their lives at any time. This situation was mostly caused by Rajah Allang, the worst of the young Sultan's uncles. He controlled the river and the land around it, and, by robbing and murdering, made the local Malays fear and obey him. They could not get away, because they had nowhere to go and no way of escaping.

Well, I told Jim about Stein's generous offer, but I also described what I knew of Patusan and the dangers involved. I watched the expression on his face change from tiredness to surprise, interest and delight.

'This is the chance I've been dreaming of! I'm so grateful to Mr Stein! But of course it's you I have to thank . . .'

I spoke quickly to stop his flow of words. 'Stein was helped when he was young, and now he wants to help *you*. And I just mentioned your name, that's all.'

He reddened, saying shyly, 'You've always trusted me.'

'That's true. But do you trust yourself?'

'I've got to prove myself. But you won't be sorry you trusted me, I promise!'

'Remember, you must decide. You are responsible for this – this plan, you and no one else.'

'Why, this is exactly what I want!'

I smiled. He was so enthusiastic! 'You see,' I said, 'you wanted to go out and shut the door behind you.'

'Did I?' he asked, looking suddenly unhappy. 'Well, you've shown me a door, haven't you?'

'Yes. If you go through it, I can promise it will be shut behind you. No one will ask what has happened to you in that distant, unknown place. You will be alone, and you will have to manage everything yourself. The outside world will forget about you completely.'

'Forget about me completely, that's it!' he whispered to himself, his eyes shining delightedly.

'Well, if you understand the conditions, you'd better find a horse and trap, and drive to Mr Stein's house as soon as possible.' And before I had finished speaking, he had run out of the room.

He did not return until next morning, because he had stayed there for dinner and the night. He could not stop talking.

'What a wonderful man Mr Stein is! And how well he speaks English! In my pocket I've got a letter for Cornelius – you know, the man I'm replacing. And look – here's a silver ring that Mr Stein has given me. It was given to him by an old Malay friend of his called Doramin. He's one of the most important chiefs in Patusan. It seems that they fought side by side when Mr Stein was there, having all those adventures, so if I show Doramin this ring, he'll help me. I think Mr Stein saved his life once – he's a brave man, isn't he? He's hoping things are all right in Patusan – he hasn't had any news for over a year, so he doesn't really know. And the river's closed, but I'm sure I'll be able to get in.'

He almost frightened me with his excited talk. After all,

he wasn't a boy going on holiday, but a grown man making a dangerous journey into the unknown. He noticed my expression, and it seemed to calm him a bit. 'You probably don't realize,' he said, 'how important the ring is to me. It means a friend, and it's a good thing to have a friend. Like you.' He paused. 'I'm going to stay there, you know.'

'If you live long enough, you'll want to come back.'

'Come back to what?' he asked absently.

'Is it to be never, then?' I asked after a moment.

'Never,' he repeated dreamily, then suddenly jumped up. 'My God! Mr Stein's ship sails in two hours' time!'

I went back to my own ship, and Jim came to say goodbye to me there. I gave him a gun and two boxes of ammunition, in case he needed them. 'The gun may help you to remain,' I said, then corrected myself quickly, 'may help you to get in, I mean.' But Jim was not troubled by this. He thanked me warmly, shouted goodbye, and jumped into his own boat. As his boatmen rowed away, I suddenly noticed he had left the ammunition behind, and I ordered my men to get a boat into the water at once. Jim was making his men row like madmen, and we could not catch him before he reached Stein's ship. In fact, our two boats arrived at the same moment.

We both stepped on to the deck, where I gave him the ammunition boxes. The ship was ready to sail. Stein's captain, a half-caste, spoke to me. He did not think Jim had any chance of survival, and was only prepared to take his passenger to the mouth of the river. 'Anybody who goes further into

'You probably don't realize how important the ring is to me,'
Jim said.

Patusan will certainly die,' he said. 'Between you and me, your friend is already a dead man.'

Then, while the captain shouted his orders, and the sails rose around us, Jim and I stood alone together on deck, shook hands, and said our last hurried words to each other. I no longer felt annoyed with him, as I had sometimes done in the past. It was clear to me what miserable danger he was going into. I believe I called him 'dear boy' and he called me 'old man'. For an unexpected, short moment we were very close.

'Don't worry,' he said. 'I promise to take care of myself. My God! Nothing can touch me. What a wonderful opportunity!'

As my boat pulled away from the ship, I saw him high up on deck, in the light of the dying sun, waving to me. I heard, 'You shall hear of me.' Because the sun was in my eyes, I couldn't see him well – it was my fate never to see him clearly – but I must say he looked very unlike a dead man to me.

6

Marlow visits Jim

The coast of Patusan is straight and dark, on a misty sea. When I arrived there, nearly two years later, I could see blue mountain tops beyond the thick green jungle. Fortunately, the river was open then, and our ship stopped at the fishing village, called Batu Kring, at the mouth of the river. We needed to take on board a native to guide our little ship up the river to the trading-post at Patusan. The man who agreed to come with us was the chief or headman of the village. He talked confidently to me (only the second white man he had ever seen), and most of his talk was about the first white man he had ever seen. He called him Tuan Jim, and spoke of him with great respect.

I thought of Jim's last words to me, 'You shall hear of me.' It was perfectly true. I was hearing of him.

At first, the headman told me, the natives had been very frightened of the lonely, white-uniformed figure, who had arrived so unexpectedly, and who gave them orders. He wanted them to take him by boat to the trading-post immediately. They were afraid Rajah Allang would be angry with them if they obeyed the stranger, but they were in greater fear of the white man's anger. After a lot of whispering among themselves, they decided that three of them would take Jim up the river by canoe.

That is how Jim entered the country where he became known and respected, from the blue mountains beyond the jungle to the white tops of the waves on the coast. Behind him were the waves of the sea, endlessly rising and sinking, and ahead of him were the immovable forests, reaching up towards the sunshine, but as dark and shadowy as life itself. And his opportunity sat waiting by his side, like an Eastern bride hiding her lovely face from her future husband.

But Jim told me later that he had never in his life felt so miserable and tired as in that canoe. He sat there, with his back straight and the sun beating down on his head, holding the gun I had given him. He felt almost sick with worry and the heat.

As soon as the canoe reached the trading-post, the three boatmen jumped out and ran off into the trees. Jim saw a stockade with high wooden posts on his left, and some native houses further away. He jumped out too, and at first seemed to be alone. But then a gate in the stockade was thrown open, and a lot of Malays ran towards him. At the same time, a boat full of men with weapons appeared on the river, so that he could not escape in the now empty canoe. There was no way out. The boatmen had handed him over to the Rajah's men.

'Luckily there was no ammunition in my gun,' Jim told me, 'so I didn't try to kill anyone, and *they* didn't hurt *me*. I just asked them what they wanted. They didn't know what

'*I simply walked in through the gate.*'

to say. Finally a servant ran up to say the Rajah wanted to see me. "All right," I said, "I want to see him too," and I simply walked in through the gate. And do you know the best thing about it? I'll tell you. It was lucky for *them* that they didn't kill me.'

He was speaking to me in front of his house on that first evening of my visit, after we had watched the moon move away over the hills, like a soul rising from a dead body. Moonlight is confusing and mysterious; it makes real things look shadowy, and shadows look real. But Jim by my side seemed very strong – not even moonlight could make him look shadowy to me. Perhaps, indeed, nothing could touch him since he had survived his fight with evil.

All was silent, all was still in this lost corner of the world. The silvery grey houses crowding along the wide shining river seemed like a line of ghostly animals, pushing forward to drink from the lifeless water. Here and there, a warm red light shone through the thin house walls, where human beings ate, and talked, and rested.

'You know,' Jim said to me, 'I often watch those little lights go out one by one. I love seeing people go to sleep under my eyes, safe and happy, with no fears for tomorrow. Peaceful here, isn't it? Ask any man, woman or child here if they trust me . . .' He paused, and spoke with deep meaning. 'Well, now I know I am all right, anyway.'

'So you've found that out at last,' I replied. 'I was always sure you were.'

'Were you?' He touched my arm lightly. 'Well, then – you

were right. My God! Just think what it means to me! How could I ever leave here? And after what you tell me of Mr Stein's offer . . . Leaving – it would be harder than dying. No, don't laugh, but I must feel – every day, every time I open my eyes – that I am trusted – that nobody can say – you know? Leave! Where would I go? Why? For what?'

I had told him (indeed it was the main reason for my visit) that Stein wanted to hand over the whole trading-post, with everything it contained, to Jim. At first Jim had refused to accept this generous offer, but I had made him realize that he had earned it. 'Stein is only giving you what you have made for yourself,' I had told him. And Jim had to give in, because all his successes, the trust, the fame, the love – all these things, which had given him control over his life and fate, had also made him a prisoner. He looked with an owner's eye at the land and its people, but it was they who owned him, to the last breath in his body.

The trust and respect of these people was something to be proud of. I, too, was proud for him. It was certainly wonderful. He had shown he was a brave, intelligent, well-organized leader of men. He clearly felt deeply and seriously about his work in Patusan – the work that had proved to him that he was 'all right'. That is why he seemed to love the land and the people with a kind of wild selfishness.

While I was in Patusan, Jim took me to visit the Rajah. 'This is where I was a prisoner for three days when I arrived,' he whispered to me, as we walked slowly through a silent and respectful crowd. 'Dirty place, isn't it? And they only gave me a small plate of rice and a bit of fried fish to eat! They took my gun away, of course, but they didn't lock me up. I was able to walk around inside the stockade.'

At that moment we arrived in front of the Rajah, and I noticed how Jim changed his way of speaking at once. His manner was calm and polite, and he spoke slowly and seriously, giving a lot of thought to his words. This had just the right effect on the evil old Rajah, who was clearly afraid of Jim, but still respected and trusted him.

Although their conversation was difficult for me to follow, I understood that Jim was acting as a kind of judge, and telling the Rajah the difference between right and wrong. Some poor villagers had been robbed while on their way to trade at Doramin's house, and it was clear that everyone knew the Rajah's men were responsible for this robbery. But to the Rajah, Doramin was a hated enemy, and the Rajah cried out suddenly, 'It's Doramin who is a thief!' His weak old body shook with anger, and all around us, his family and servants stared, their mouths open.

Then Jim began to speak. 'Nobody,' he said calmly, 'should prevent any man from getting his food and his children's food honestly. Nobody should ever steal.' There was a great stillness in the room. Finally the old Rajah looked up, shaking his head tiredly, and said, 'You hear, my people! No more of these little games.'

One of his servants came forward to offer us two cups of coffee. 'You needn't drink,' Jim whispered quickly to me.

I didn't understand what he meant at first, but just watched

53

him as he drank. Then I realized, and felt extremely annoyed. 'Why the hell do you put me in danger like this?' I whispered back to him, smiling pleasantly all the time. I drank the coffee, of course – I couldn't avoid doing that – and we left soon afterwards.

'I'm very sorry about that,' said Jim quietly to me as we walked back to our boat. 'I really don't think he would try to poison us. Personally, I never think about it. You see, if I want to do any good here, I have to show I don't care about the danger. Many people trust me to do that – for them.'

'But anyone can see he's afraid of you,' I said crossly, all the time watching for the first sign of stomach pain.

'That's just it! He's probably afraid of me because I'm not afraid of his coffee.' He pointed to part of the stockade, where the tops of several posts were broken. 'Look, that's where I jumped over, on my third day as a prisoner. The Rajah and his advisers had spent all the time since my arrival trying to decide what to do with me, and I had just been waiting for something to happen. But suddenly I realized what extreme danger I was in, so I just ran at the stockade, and flew over like a bird. I picked myself up on the other side and ran as fast as I could towards the village houses, about four hundred metres away. Behind me I could hear shouting, as the Rajah's men started to follow me. Ahead of me was a creek. I jumped across it and landed in very soft, wet mud. I couldn't move my legs at all, and lay there, trying desperately to pull myself out with my arms. The mud came right up to my chin, and as I dug wildly, I thought I was burying myself even deeper. I was becoming exhausted, but I made one last great attempt – and at last felt myself creeping weakly out of the mud on the other side of the creek. Think of me, muddy and alone, in that terrible place, with no friends or anyone to help me! I ran through the village – women and children ran screaming from me, men stood still, staring at me in horror – I don't suppose I looked at all like a human being.

'Finally, I turned a corner, and fell into the arms of several surprised-looking men. I just had breath to cry, "Doramin!" They carried me to Doramin's house, which was inside its own stockade, and put me down in front of a large, important-looking man, sitting in a chair. Somewhere in my muddy clothes I managed to find Stein's silver ring. Everyone was shouting excitedly, and running here and there. I could hear shots in the distance from the Rajah's men, but here I was safe. Doramin's people were closing the heavy gates of the stockade, and giving me water to drink. Doramin's wife took care of me – she was very kind to me.'

About sixty families in Patusan considered Doramin their chief. His men frequently had fights with the Rajah's people, mostly about trading. The problem was that the Rajah thought he alone should trade in Patusan; he became wild with anger when he discovered anyone else buying or selling. He was a cruel, evil and cowardly man, who had made a habit of robbing and killing Doramin's people, until Jim came.

There was a third leader in Patusan, an Arab half-caste called Sherif Ali, who had persuaded some of the natives to join him. They lived high up on the top of one of the two mountains, and from there often came down at night to steal food and animals, kill people and burn buildings. Parts of the countryside were blackened and empty, and the local people were suffering badly. In this confused situation, none of the three leaders trusted or respected each other, and until

'They put me down in front of a large, important-looking man.'

Jim's arrival, there seemed no way of bringing peace to
the country.

If you once saw Doramin, you would never forget him.
He was much larger than most Malays, with a heavy body
dressed in richly coloured clothes, and a big, flat, round head,
with proud, staring eyes. No one ever heard him raise his
voice. He never moved without help; when he walked, two
strong young men dressed in white held his elbows. In the
afternoons, he sat silently by his wife's side, looking out,
through an opening in the stockade, at the dark green jungle,
the distant purple mountains, and the silver shining river.

This old couple had a son called Dain Waris, a polite,
handsome young man of twenty-four or five. They loved him
deeply, although they never showed it. I liked him as soon as
I met him. I realized he was both brave and intelligent, and I
believe he trusted and even understood Jim. 'Dain Waris is
the best friend I ever had, except for you,' Jim told me proudly.
'We fought together, you know. Against Sherif Ali. You see,
when I arrived, the Rajah, Doramin and Sherif Ali were all
afraid of each other. I soon realized what I had to do, but I
needed Dain Waris's help. He was the first to believe in me,
and he persuaded his father to agree to my plan.'

Jim's plan! I heard the whole story of it from him during
my visit. He had decided that it was necessary to defeat Sherif
Ali, and planned to attack his mountain home. Doramin
owned several heavy old guns, used in the past for fighting
jungle wars. One dark night, Jim arranged for teams of men
using ropes to pull these guns right up to the top of one of the

mountains. It was difficult, hot work, and all the time Jim and the men were lifting and pulling, old Doramin sat watching silently in his chair. The Malays already believed that Jim was doing the impossible. How could those guns, too heavy for one man to lift, reach the mountain top? This was the beginning of their great respect for Jim.

From there, Doramin's men had an excellent view of the other mountain top, where Sherif Ali and his followers were asleep. As soon as the sun rose, the first shots were fired, on Jim's order, and the battle began. Jim, with Dain Waris by his side, led a group up the second hill towards Sherif Ali's

stockade. He knew he had to win this fight – Doramin's people were depending on him. He and Dain Waris were the first to break into the Arab's stockade. Close behind them came Tamb' Itam, Jim's personal servant and a fearless fighter. He was a Malay from the north, a stranger to Patusan, who for a time had been a prisoner of the Rajah. When he escaped, he came to Jim, and ever since had followed him everywhere, like a shadow.

The battle was violent, but short. The stockade was burnt down and Sherif Ali and his men were defeated. Some were dead, but most of them were chased away into the jungle.

Jim led a group towards Sherif Ali's stockade.

When this wonderful news reached the village, people were delighted. They ran in and out of their houses, shouting, singing and laughing excitedly. Of course Jim was delighted too. He had succeeded in doing what he had promised, and now he could believe in himself again. I can't tell you how completely lonely he appeared to me, but somehow his loneliness added to his greatness. He seemed to be one of those men who can only be measured by the greatness of their fame, and his fame, remember, was the greatest thing for many a day's journey around, even beyond the jungle. His word was the one truth of every passing day, and reports of his fame travelled far and wide, heard on the lips of whispering men, full of wonder and mystery.

No one ever saw Sherif Ali again, and when some of his men crept back from the jungle later, it was Jim, advised by Dain Waris, who chose a headman from among them. The Rajah was afraid that Jim would attack him too – he could lose his land, his money, his women, his servants! – and therefore he behaved very carefully. So Jim found himself in complete control of one of the most dangerous corners of the world.

Old Doramin, however, had a secret wish. He wanted to see his son take the Rajah's place one day, and just before I left, he spoke to me about it. 'Of course Tuan Jim knows best,' he said, 'but if I could only have a promise! I worry about the future of our country. You see, the land is always here, but white men come and go. One day this white man, too, will—'

'No, no,' I replied quickly, without thinking. 'He won't go.'

Doramin looked into my face. 'That is good news indeed,' he answered calmly. 'But why do you say that?'

And his wife, a small, thin, motherly woman, asked sadly, 'Why did he travel so far away from his home? Has he no family, no old mother, who will always remember his face?'

I could not answer. Strangely enough, that evening, my last in Patusan, I was asked the same question again.

7

Jim in love, and in danger

This brings me to the story of his love. Remember the unspeakably awful Cornelius? I saw him and spoke to him myself, as he crept around Patusan with evil in his heart, and lying promises on his lips. How his poor wife had come to marry him is a mystery to me. I do not know, either, what had happened to her daughter's father, who was not Cornelius. The fact remains that she already had her daughter when she married the Portuguese. Bitterly disappointed with his life, he seemed to hate the woman and her child, and behaved very badly to both of them. The two women lived very lonely lives at the trading-post, with no other friends or companions. When the older woman died, a short time before Jim's arrival, the daughter was lonelier than ever.

Jim decided to leave Doramin's place after only a few days there, and move into the house at the trading-post, where Cornelius and the girl lived. Although Doramin warned him this would be dangerous, Jim felt it was his duty to take care of Stein's business. At first Cornelius pretended to be delighted that Jim was staying with him, but he soon showed his real character. Jim realized that Cornelius had been stealing from Stein at every opportunity. There seemed to be almost nothing left of the business, and some of the papers were missing.

'It was miserable there,' Jim told me. 'Cornelius was too mean to give me any regular meals. And then I heard the Rajah was planning to murder me! Pleasant, wasn't it?' He added that he didn't know what made him stay there for six weeks, but of course we can guess. He was very sorry for the motherless girl. It appears Cornelius frequently shouted at her, although he was too cowardly to hit her.

'Call me father, and with respect, too,' he used to scream into her face. 'Your mother was an evil woman, and you're evil as well!' The girl usually put her hands over her ears and ran away, while Cornelius chased her, shouting wildly and often throwing dirt at her. But sometimes she used to listen in silence, staring scornfully at him and replying with a poisonous word or two. Jim told me he could not leave the house while the poor girl was so unhappy; his conscience would not let him. But every day he received another message that there were plans to drown, shoot or poison him, and he realized he was in great danger. He no longer slept well at night. He noticed that Cornelius was acting very strangely, giving hesitating answers to Jim's questions, creeping secretly round the house in the dark, and having mysterious meetings with people at night.

One night, however, Jim was woken by the girl. She was holding a burning torch high above his head, and was whispering, 'Get up! Get up!' He jumped to his feet and she put his gun into his hand. 'Can you fight four men?' she asked.

He answered politely, 'Certainly – whatever you want,'

and followed her outside. On the veranda he noticed that Cornelius's bed was empty.

The girl led him away from the house towards the trading-post buildings. She turned and whispered to Jim, 'They were going to attack you while you slept.'

Jim felt miserably disappointed. He did not want to hear any more about these attempts to kill him. He had only come outside with her because he thought she wanted his help. But they walked on together. It was a beautiful night, quite cool, with a soft wind blowing from the river. Remember, my friends, this is a love story I am telling you now.

The girl stopped outside one of the buildings and held her torch up high like a flag. 'They're in there, waiting for the sign,' she whispered. 'But you have been sleeping so restlessly. I watch you every night.'

'You've been watching me?' Jim felt first surprised, then delighted. But at that moment a movement caught his eye, and he saw a dark figure move quickly past. 'Cornelius!' he called in a strong voice. There was a deep silence.

'Run! Go to Doramin!' the girl said, excitedly. 'For the moment you are safe – they know you're awake, they know you're big, strong, fearless – but what about tomorrow? Or any other night? How can I always be watching?'

Jim was terribly touched by the feeling in her voice. He realized that the only escape from his loneliness was – in her. If he went away from her, he told me, it would be the end of everything. So the only thing to do was to enter the building and find his murderers.

'How can I always be watching?' the girl said.

He moved forward, and the girl, understanding his plan, ran round to the side of the building, and put her torch through the open window, so that he had enough light to see.

Jim threw open the door and went in. From a dark corner a man ran towards him, holding a knife. Jim shot him in the head and killed him. Three more men came forward, holding out their empty hands to show they had no weapons. 'Walk outside!' Jim ordered. At the door he was joined by the girl, still holding the torch. Her black hair fell to her waist, and her white dress touched the ground as she walked.

The three men walked in front, followed by Jim and the girl, until they reached the river. 'Jump!' shouted Jim, and the men jumped. Jim watched them swim into the distance. He turned to the girl. His heart seemed suddenly to grow too big for his chest, and he was unable to speak. They looked at each other for a long time, then she threw the burning torch far into the river. The calm soft starlight came down on them; it was one of those nights that seem made for love. I don't suppose he could express himself very well, but there are moments when our souls need silence more than words.

I met the girl, of course, on my visit. She had a child's sensitive face, and moved quickly and lightly, like a little bird. Her skin was smooth and her hair a deep blue-black, flowing thickly on to her lovely shoulders. She spoke and understood quite a lot of English, and used to listen carefully to our conversations, keeping her big clear eyes fastened on our lips. Her love for Jim surrounded him completely; I felt I could almost touch it. I suppose you think I, too, am romantic, but I'm just telling you what I saw. I realized she loved him deeply and jealously, but what she was jealous of, I did not know. After all, the land, the people, the forests were on her side, guarding Jim day and night and keeping him prisoner. Even Tamb' Itam, ready to die for the Tuan, was proud to guard

Jim. And the girl herself, I believe, never went to sleep until Jim and I had separated for the night. More than once I saw her and Jim, through the window of my room, stand quietly together on the veranda – two figures very close, his arm around her waist, her head on his shoulder.

He called her Jewel. Pretty, isn't it? A strange name, of course, but it probably explained the surprising story I had heard on my way to Patusan, in a village about three hundred kilometres south of there. Local people told me that the mysterious white stranger who had taken control of the area had discovered a very large and valuable jewel. As he was often seen walking with a girl, behaving with great respect and care towards her, it was supposed that she wore the white man's jewel hidden in her dress. It was true that Jim took the girl on evening walks, and that romance had taken hold of him, but the rest of the story was just imagination. He did not hide his jewel; in fact, he was extremely proud of it.

'I – I love her dearly,' he told me. 'You see, it's so wonderful when you feel you're *needed* by someone. And her life was so awful before! She trusts me to take care of her. And I will! You know, I've been here only two years now, and I really can't imagine living anywhere else. The thought of the world outside is enough to frighten me, because—' and he looked down at his boots '—I haven't forgotten why I came here. Not yet!' We walked by the river in silence for a few moments. 'Isn't it strange that all these people, who would do anything for me, will never understand? If you asked them who is brave, who is faithful, who they would trust with their lives . . . They would say, Tuan Jim. But they can never know the real, real truth.' He paused again. 'It doesn't matter. I am – almost – happy with what I've done. And they believe in me – that's what *they've* done for *me*. I shall always remain here.'

When he left me, I saw the girl's white figure coming towards me. She had clearly been waiting for this opportunity. She wanted something simple but impossible – a promise, an explanation. Because she had grown up in Patusan and knew nothing of the strange world outside, her one great fear was that Jim, who had come from there, would one day return to it. She had watched us closely and listened to all our conversations, afraid perhaps that I was planning to take Jim away from her. And now she spoke to me, desperate to know what her fate would be. I was deeply touched by her helplessness; she was young, beautiful, and very unhappy.

'He promised he would never leave me,' she whispered, holding her lovely head in her hands.

'Why don't you believe him?' I replied. '*I* certainly won't take him away.'

'They always leave us,' she said, even more quietly. 'I don't want to suffer like my mother. She cried bitterly while she was dying. My father also promised never to leave, you know.'

'Ah! but Jim isn't like that,' I said. She was silent; it seemed strange to me. 'What has he been telling you?'

'I don't know!' she cried miserably. 'He says there's something he can never forget! What is it? Tell me! You both remember something! Is it alive? Is it dead? I hate it! Will it come for him? Will he see it in his sleep, perhaps, when he cannot see me, and then leave me? Will it be a sign – a call?'

I was deeply moved by her pain. I wanted very much to bring calm to her soul, and to say, 'Have no fear!' But how do you kill fear? Can you shoot a ghost through the heart, can you cut off its head? I spoke with a heavy heart, with a kind of anger. 'There is nothing in that unknown world outside, no face, no voice, no one alive or dead who can take Jim away from you.'

'He told me that,' she answered softly. 'But why did you come? You make me afraid. Do you – do you want him?'

'I shall never come again,' I said bitterly. 'And I don't want him. No one wants him. This world you don't know is too big to miss him. And you've got his heart in your hand. You must feel that. You must know that.'

'Yes, I know that,' she whispered, hard and still, like a figure in stone.

I was getting excited. I felt I almost had a chance of killing the ghost at last. 'In the whole world there is no one who will ever need his heart, his head, his hand! From all the millions of people out there, I can tell you that as long as he lives, there will never come a call or a sign for him! Never! Why are you afraid? You know he's strong, faithful and brave. He is more than that. He has greatness – and the world doesn't want him, it has forgotten him!'

I stopped. There was a deep silence over Patusan.

'Why?' she asked quietly. I felt the ghost escaping, and, confused, did not answer. 'Why?' she repeated. 'Tell me!'

Suddenly I cried out angrily, 'Because he is not good enough.'

69

'That is what he said,' she replied scornfully. 'You lie!'

'Listen!' I cried. 'Nobody, nobody is good enough . . .'

She turned away. How could I explain? He had told her and she had not believed him. Who knows if we both lied or not?

But none of that mattered. You see, I had decided that Jim, who was the only one I really cared about, had at last taken control of his fate. He had told me he was – almost – happy with what he'd done. Not many of us can say that. Can any of you here? No, I thought not. So it did not matter who trusted him, who loved him, who hated him.

The next morning Jim came with me on the first part of my journey out of Patusan. As our canoe moved fast down the river, the trading-post and the houses disappeared behind us.

'That man Cornelius hates you,' I said, remembering a recent conversation with the Portuguese. 'He thinks you've stolen everything from him. He could be dangerous.'

'My dear Marlow, I feel that if I go straight, nothing can touch me. Everything depends on me, and my God! I know I can do it. Cornelius isn't worth worrying about.'

The air was hot and heavy, and smelt of mud. We were silent for a time, knowing we would separate soon. Suddenly the sky seemed to widen, there was a freshness in the air, and at last we were out of the jungle. Ahead of us was the open sea. I breathed deeply, I felt free again. The girl was right. There was a sign, a call from the wider world outside, for me!

'This is wonderful!' I cried, then looked at the unfortunate man beside me. He sat with his head bent low on his chest, and did not look up, perhaps afraid to see what his romantic conscience had written on the clear sky.

I remember the smallest details of that afternoon. We landed on a white beach, near the mouth of the river, to wait for my ship. Two natives came to tell Jim that the Rajah's men were stealing their eggs. He told them gently to wait, and they sat down obediently on the ground.

'You see, I can't go away,' he said to me. 'The people here need me now. They would fight among themselves if I left. I must stay. I shall be faithful.' I remembered Stein's words – *follow the dream, to the end.* 'And there's Jewel,' he went on. 'She's everything to me. When shall you and I meet again, I wonder?'

'Never – unless you come out,' I replied. He didn't seem very surprised. He was quiet for a while.

'Goodbye, then,' he said after a pause. 'Perhaps it's best this way.' We shook hands, and I walked to the ship's boat, which by now was waiting for me in shallow water.

'Will you go home again soon?' asked Jim, just as I was getting in.

'In a year or so, if I am alive then,' I said.

The boat started moving away from the beach. Jim, at the water's edge, spoke louder. 'Tell them . . .' he began. I ordered the boatmen to stop rowing, and waited. Tell who? 'No – nothing,' he said, and waved us away. I did not look at the beach again until I had climbed on board the ship.

By that time the sun had gone down and the coast looked very black, but I could still see Jim on the beach. The two

'I must stay. I shall be faithful.'

natives were standing close to him, no doubt telling the white lord about their miserable, difficult lives, and he was listening patiently. They soon disappeared in the growing darkness, but Jim remained, white from head to foot. He had the sea at his feet, and the opportunity by his side – still hidden from him. What do you think, my friends? Was it still hidden? For me that white figure in the stillness of coast and sea seemed to stand at the heart of a great mystery, catching all the light left in a darkened world . . . And then, suddenly, I lost him . . .

8

The end of the story

With these words Marlow finished speaking, and the men around him got up from their armchairs. They did not seem to want to discuss the story, although it was incomplete. And only one of these listeners ever heard the last word of the story. It came to him more than two years later, in a thick packet containing many pages of writing. He had returned to dark, rainy England, and knew he would never go back to the East, but the packet made him think of distant seas under a bright, hot sun, and faces and voices from the past.

He opened Marlow's letter to him, and began to read.

———————— ✳ ————————

I don't suppose you've forgotten Jim. You alone have shown interest in him, although you did not agree that he was in control of his fate. Well, you must judge for yourself now. Here is Jim's last message to the world – a greyish piece of paper, on which he wrote simply, 'An awful thing has happened', and then, 'I must now at once . . .' Nothing more. I imagine he could not describe the true horror of what he saw. I can understand that. I also send you an old letter, which was found carefully put away in his desk. It is from his father, and Jim probably received it a few days before joining the *Patna*. The good old vicar writes four pages of fatherly advice and family news; the mother and daughters send all their love to their sailor son and brother. Jim never answered it, but he kept it lovingly all those years. Who knows what conversations his suffering soul had with those clear-eyed, ghostly figures, living their peaceful lives in that quiet corner of the world?

And in the rest of this letter I will tell you the end of Jim's story. It is a real adventure, romantic beyond the wildest dreams of his boyhood, but with an ending that seems in some way unavoidable. Something like this had to happen. I have found out almost all the details, but I wonder how Jim himself would tell the story. It is hard for me to believe that I shall never hear his voice again, or see his fresh, young, excited face.

About a year ago I arrived at Samarang, and went to visit Stein as usual. I was surprised and pleased to see Tamb' Itam, Jim's servant, at Stein's house, and hoped that perhaps Jim had come on a visit. But as soon as I met Stein, I realized something was wrong. The old man was looking miserable.

'Come and see the girl,' he said sadly. 'They arrived two days ago. It's terrible! Terrible! You must talk to her, make her forgive him. Young hearts do not forgive easily.' Refusing to say any more, he absolutely pushed me through a door.

I found myself in a large, cool room. The girl was sitting at a long table, resting her head on her arms. She opened her eyes and recognized me at once. I felt cold to the bone as I looked at her hard, sad face and her black, staring eyes.

'He has left me,' she said quietly. 'I wanted to die with him! But he refused! Ah, you men are unfaithful! What makes you so bad? I shall never cry for him! Not one tear! He could see my face, hear my voice! And he still went away from me! Driven by some evil thing he had heard or seen in his sleep . . .'

I was bitterly disappointed. 'You must forgive him,' I said. 'We all want forgiveness.' My voice sounded strange to me. Her frozen face did not change, and she made no sign as I left the room. I was glad to escape, and went to find Tamb' Itam, who told me as much of the story as he knew.

It all began with a man called Captain Brown, one of the most evil seamen in the Western Pacific. From Cape York to Eden Bay he was famous for cheating, robbing and murdering; he was a cruel, violent and proud man, with no idea of duty, conscience or honour. At this moment in his life he was also desperate, because he had not earned much from his recent adventures, and his men were hungry and tired. They had stolen a Spanish ship, and were sailing it across the Java Sea, towards the Indian Ocean, when suddenly Brown realized that Patusan would be a good place to get food and water. Perhaps he had heard of it, as a largeish village up the river, or perhaps it was just a name on his map. Anyway, they left their ship at the mouth of the river, and took the ship's boat up to the trading-post. However, the headman of the fishing village at Batu Kring had managed to warn the Patusan people, who started firing their guns as soon as Brown's boat appeared. Brown angrily ordered his men to fire back; he had not been expecting a fight. He noticed the creek (which Jim had jumped over in his escape from the Rajah's men), and told his men to row into it. They landed, and climbed a small hill, which gave them a good view of the village and the Rajah's stockade. They cut down some trees to make their own stockade, and waited for the natives to attack, in the growing darkness.

The people of Patusan were frightened and confused. Their white lord was away in another part of the country, so it was Dain Waris who had ordered the shooting. Women and children left their homes and crowded into Jim's house, where Jewel was in control. She also kept the ammunition, while Jim was absent. Doramin, his son, Jewel, the Rajah's adviser Kassim, and all the local chiefs and headmen met in Jim's house to decide what to do. Jewel and Dain Waris wanted to drive away the white men, but Doramin only seemed interested in keeping his son safe. Kassim was playing a clever game, hoping that these white men would attack and defeat Doramin's men before Jim returned. Meanwhile he smiled and listened, pretending to offer the Rajah's help against the white men.

Part of Kassim's plan involved Cornelius, because he spoke English. So the next day Kassim and Cornelius went to talk to Brown in his stockade. Brown listened to these offers of help and began to feel more hopeful. He had come to Patusan just to steal food, but perhaps here was an opportunity for him. Perhaps he could take control of Patusan, and make himself a rich man. He would work with this white man they called Tuan Jim, for a while anyway – until it became necessary to kill him. This indeed was Cornelius's advice. 'You must kill him as soon as you can,' he said repeatedly. 'Then you can have everything!'

While this was happening, Dain Waris's canoes went silently down to an island at the mouth of the river. This was on Doramin's orders, in order to cut off Brown's escape route back to his ship, but also, I suspect, to keep his son out of harm's way. Kassim sent food to Brown and his men, but did not tell them about the canoes.

Later that day Brown saw from his stockade one of the villagers walking out of a house. He gave an order to one of his men, who fired a single shot. The native fell to the ground, dead. 'That's right!' cried Brown delightedly. 'Put the fear of sudden death in them!'

Darkness fell, and soon one of the white men decided to go back to the boat to get his pipe. When he reached the creek, there was a bang, and he cried out in pain, 'I've been hit!' Brown and the others listened to him dying slowly in the mud for several hours; they knew they could not help him.

At last it was morning, and Brown saw a group of Malays coming towards the creek, with a tall white man in the middle of them. Jim had returned to Patusan during the night, to the great happiness of the villagers, and was coming to talk to Brown. 'He'll come and order you to leave his people alone,' Cornelius had told Brown.

Soon Jim left the villagers behind and came on alone. Brown went down to the creek to meet him. He knew at once that he and Jim would never understand each other. Jim's

*Jim left the villagers behind and came on alone,
and Brown went down to the creek to meet him.*

clean white clothes, his honest eyes, and confident look made Brown hate him immediately. They spoke to each other, two men completely opposite in character, separated only by a muddy creek. Most of the time Jim listened, while Brown talked, choosing his words carefully. He knew nothing of Jim's past, but he was extremely clever at finding the weakest place in a man's soul, and, by an evil chance, he found his way to Jim's.

'You can't blame me for shooting that native last night!' he cried. 'If you have to save your own life in the dark, you don't care how many other people die, do you? I know I've done wrong in the past, but what about you? Why did you come and bury yourself here? You're no better than I am! Don't be a coward! There are two hundred of you to every one of us. Either come and fight us, or let us go!'

Jim's face was like thunder. Finally, after a long silence, he replied, 'Well, if you promise to leave the coast, we will let you go, and not fire on you unless you fire first.' He turned away.

The conversation was at an end, and Jim went back to the village to speak to Doramin and the headmen. Some of them were doubtful about allowing the white men to leave. 'They are cruel, evil robbers, who have killed one of us!' they cried. 'We should kill them!'

But Jim said gently, 'They have done evil things, certainly; but fortune has not been kind to them. Men can act badly sometimes, and still not be completely evil. It is best to let them go with their lives.' He paused, then went on, 'Have I ever given you bad advice? Trust me. I am ready to answer with my life for any harm that comes to you if the white men are allowed to go.'

All the headmen gave their opinion. Most of them simply said, 'We believe Tuan Jim. We will do what he advises.'

And so it was agreed. Brown and his men were allowed to leave the hill, get into their boat, and row out of the creek into the river.

That evening Jim sent Tamb' Itam down the river with a message for Dain Waris. 'Tell him that his men must not fire at the whites when they leave. That is the agreement here.'

'It is an important message,' said Tamb' Itam. 'Give me a sign for Dain Waris, so that he knows these words come from you.'

Ever since Jim came to Patusan, he had worn Stein's silver ring. Everyone knew the ring, as it had been Doramin's present to Stein long ago. Jim now took it off his finger and gave it to Tamb' Itam, as a sign for Dain Waris.

The next morning Jim stood outside the Rajah's stockade, watching Brown and his men leave Patusan, in a thick grey mist. But on board Brown's boat was the evil Cornelius, hiding under a sail. He was disappointed that Brown had not killed Jim, and he had decided to take his revenge in a different way. He had promised to show Brown another creek, which led to the small island further down the river, where Doramin's son and his men were waiting with their canoes. It was easy for Brown, who saw the chance to take revenge for his own misfortunes. Dain Waris and his men, with Tamb'

Itam, were watching the bigger creek, and did not expect anyone to attack from the narrow creek behind them. When Brown's men fired their guns, several natives fell, including Dain Waris, who was shot through the head. The others ran away, screaming with fear. The white robbers were never seen again in Patusan, but it was known that their ship sank in the Indian Ocean a month later.

Cornelius also died, because Tamb' Itam saw him on the island and realized what he had done. The narrow creek was impossible to find without help from someone who knew it. Cornelius tried to escape, but Tamb' Itam killed him with his knife. This done, Tamb' Itam hurried back to his canoe, to take news of the disaster to his lord.

At first Jim was angry. He wanted to chase the robbers, and began to give orders about collecting men and boats, but Tamb' Itam hesitated.

'Forgive me, Tuan,' he said, ashamed, 'but it is not safe for me, your servant, to go among the people.'

Then Jim understood the awful truth. He had run away from one world, and now his new world, the one he had made with his own hands, was falling around him. He sat silently like a stone figure, while Tamb' Itam talked of fighting, and the girl talked of danger. Who can tell what thoughts passed through his head? I think it was then that he tried to write – to somebody – and could not finish the message. Loneliness was closing on him. People had trusted him with their lives, but they would never be able to understand him.

Meanwhile in the village there was great sadness, and

anger, as the body of the chief's son was brought home by canoe. Doramin looked at his dead son, and slowly, very slowly, took Jim's silver ring off the cold, stiff hand. The crowd cried out in horror when they saw that well-known ring, and Doramin suddenly let out a great violent shout, deep from the chest, like a wounded animal – a cry of pain and anger. Then there was silence.

At about this time, Jim left his house and started walking towards the river. 'Time to finish this,' he said.

The girl followed him, calling out, 'Won't you fight?'

'There is nothing to fight for,' he replied.

'Won't you escape?' she cried again.

'There is no escape,' he said.

'So you are leaving? Don't you remember you promised you would never leave me?'

'Enough, poor girl,' he answered. 'If I stayed, I would not be worth having.'

She ran to him, and, crying bitterly, held him in her arms. 'I shall hold you like this! You are mine!'

Jim pulled himself away, looked into her face for a long moment, then ran to the water's edge. He jumped into a canoe, with Tamb' Itam, and as they moved away, the girl screamed, 'You are unfaithful!'

'Forgive me!' he cried.

'Never!' she called back. 'Never!'

When Jim arrived at Doramin's stockade, the crowd of crying, confused people separated, respectfully and fearfully, to allow him to enter. He walked slowly through them, right

up to the old chief, who was sitting in his usual chair, with a
gun on his knees. Doramin's wife was bending miserably over
her son's body, which was covered with a sheet. Jim lifted
the sheet to look at his dead friend, then dropped it without
a word. He waited for a moment, then said gently, 'I am
responsible. I come in sadness, with no weapon. I am ready.'

The heavy old man was helped up from his chair, and the
silver ring, which Jim had worn so proudly, fell to the floor.
With an expression of mad pain and anger on his face,

Doramin stared at Jim standing in front of him.

Doramin stared at Jim standing stiffly in front of him. Then, looking him straight in the eyes, he lifted his gun and shot his son's friend through the chest. Jim looked proudly and bravely round at all the staring faces, then, with a hand over his lips, he fell forward, dead.

And that's the end. He disappears under a cloud, mysterious, forgotten, and much too romantic. Perhaps in that last, short moment he saw the face of his opportunity, waiting for him like an Eastern bride. He left the arms of a living woman who loved him, to marry the shadowy ghost of imagined honour and duty. Is he completely happy now, I wonder? We ought to know; he is one of us. Was I so very wrong, after all, to believe in him? Who knows? He is gone, and the poor girl is living a soundless, frozen life in Stein's house. Stein looks much older now, and is feeling his age. He often says he is 'preparing to leave all this', while he waves his hand sadly at his butterflies.

GLOSSARY

ammunition pieces of metal fired from a gun, e.g. bullets

anger the feeling of being angry

area a district or region, part of a country

attack to start fighting or hurting someone

bear *(v)* to accept something difficult or unpleasant without complaining

bitter showing sadness, anger or disappointment

bride a woman on or just before her wedding day

bridge (on a ship) a raised platform, usually enclosed, from where the ship is controlled and steered by the captain and officers

butterfly an insect with large, usually brightly coloured wings

canoe a light narrow boat moved by paddles

conscience knowing in your mind what is right or wrong about your own actions

court the place where judges and lawyers listen to law cases

coward someone who shows fear or weakness in dangerous or unpleasant situations

creek a small, narrow stream or river

creep *(v)* to move slowly, quietly or secretly, close to the ground

deck any of the floors of a ship

duty what you do or should do in your life or work

encourage to give someone hope, support, confidence

evil wicked, very bad

faithful that you can trust, e.g. a faithful friend

fame being well known

fate what will happen in the future

fire (a gun) *(v)* to shoot with a gun

forehead the part of your face above the eyes

forgive to say or show that you are not angry with someone any more

guano bird droppings used to make the earth richer for growing plants

guilty having done wrong, or feeling that you have done wrong

half-caste a person who has parents of different races

hand over to give or give back something, often unwillingly

hell the worst place you can imagine; in some religions, the place where bad people go after they die

hero (*adj* **heroic**) a very brave man, or the most important male character in a story

honour a person's good name; respect for a person

imagination making pictures in your mind

inquiry a court case to find out why a disaster happened

jewel a beautiful and valuable stone

jungle a thick forest in a hot country

lord a man of noble family, or a trusted leader

master's certificate a piece of paper showing that someone has passed the necessary exams to be in charge of a ship

mate (**on a ship**) an officer who assists the captain

merchant navy ships (and the sailors who work in them) that carry goods from country to country

mud (*adj* **muddy**) soft, wet earth

native (*n*) someone born in a place, country, etc.

on board on the ship

official (*n & adj*) someone who does important work, especially for the government

opportunity a chance, the right time for doing something

pepper a hot-tasting powder made from a plant, which is put on food

pilgrim someone who travels a long way to a place of religious importance

poison *(v)* to put something in someone's food or drink to make them ill or kill them

port *(n)* a harbour, a safe place for ships to arrive and depart

Rajah a native Asian prince, a local leader or nobleman

respect *(v)* to have a good opinion of someone

romantic *(n)* someone who likes dreaming, imagining an ideal world

scornful feeling or showing that someone or something is bad or worthless

shame an unhappy feeling because you have done something wrong or stupid

sink *(v)* to go down in the water

soul the part of you that does not die with your body

stockade a line or wall of strong wooden posts, surrounding an area

suffer to feel pain or great sadness

Sultan an important native prince or leader

torch a small lamp or burning stick to give light in the darkness

trading-post a place where goods are bought and sold, in an area far from any shops or towns

trap (horse and trap) a small carriage for one or two people, with a horse and driver

trust to feel sure that someone is good and honest; to believe in someone

veranda a platform with an open front and a roof around the sides of a house, where people in hot countries often sit in the shade

vicar a priest in the Church of England

Before Reading

1 **Read the story introduction on the first page of the book, and the back cover. What do you know now about Jim? Choose T (True) or F (False) for each of these sentences.**

1 Jim is delighted to become a sailor. T/F

2 He is made captain of the *Patna*. T/F

3 He always does his duty as a brave man. T/F

4 No one believes in Jim after the accident. T/F

5 Later on, Jim tells his story to his friends. T/F

6 Jim goes to live in south-east Asia. T/F

2 **Can you guess what happens to Jim in the story? Circle Y (Yes) or N (No) for each of these possibilities.**

1 When the accident happens, Jim . . .

   a) hesitates too long before giving an order. Y/N

   b) saves himself first. Y/N

   c) kills someone. Y/N

   d) escapes from a ship that is about to sink. Y/N

   e) leaves drowning men to die in the sea. Y/N

2 In the search for his lost honour, Jim . . .

   a) discovers he is brave after all. Y/N

   b) becomes even more disappointed with himself. Y/N

   c) has a great adventure. Y/N

   d) ends his life, friendless and unloved. Y/N

   e) is considered a hero by all around him. Y/N

ACTIVITIES

While Reading

Read Chapter 1, and answer these questions.

1 Why was Jim popular in the Eastern ports?
2 Why do you think Jim didn't want people to know his other name?
3 Who called him Lord Jim?
4 What was Jim's family like?
5 What happened one stormy night on the training ship?
6 Where was the *Patna* going, and why?
7 What do you think happened to the *Patna* at the end of Chapter 1, and what do you think will happen next?

Read Chapters 2 and 3. Who said this, and to whom? Who or what were they talking about?

1 'I didn't think of danger just then.'
2 'Don't be too quick to judge him.'
3 'We should put an end to this now.'
4 'I won't let anyone call me names outside this court.'
5 'It is – hell.'
6 'Do you think you can?'
7 'Nothing could save them!'
8 'I'm going to get away.'
9 'It seems you did.'
10 'I'd jumped into an everlasting deep hole . . .'

Before you read Chapter 4, what do you think of Jim's actions so far? Think about or discuss these questions.

1 What was Jim guilty of?
2 Were there any good reasons for what he did?
3 Should he be punished? If so, how? If not, why not?
4 Was anyone else more at fault than Jim? If so, who, and how should they be punished?
5 Do you think Jim is brave, or cowardly, or a bit of both?

Read Chapters 4 and 5. Are these sentences true (T) or false (F)? Rewrite the false sentences with the correct information.

1 The inquiry court decided not to punish Jim in any way.
2 A man called Chester offered Jim a job on a guano island.
3 Marlow promised Jim a job on his own ship.
4 Jim always left his job if the *Patna* was mentioned.
5 Stein was scornful of Jim's problem and refused to help.
6 In Jim's time, most people in the East knew Patusan well.
7 Stein sent Jim to Patusan as manager of his trading-post.
8 Marlow was not sure how Jim's character would develop.
9 Patusan was a safe place because of the Sultan's uncle, who controlled the area and who was kind to the local Malays.
10 Jim was planning to stay in Patusan for a very short time.

Read Chapters 6 and 7. Choose the best question-word for these questions, and then answer them.

Who / Why
1 . . . was Jim happy with his work in Patusan?

2 ... were Rajah Allang, Doramin, and Sherif Ali?

3 ... was the first person in Patusan to believe in Jim?

4 ... was Jim delighted after the attack on Sherif Ali?

5 ... did Jim move into the house at the trading-post?

6 ... saved Jim from being attacked in his bed?

7 ... did local people talk about the discovery of a jewel?

8 ... did the girl speak privately to Marlow?

9 ... did Marlow warn Jim about?

10 ... did Jim feel he had to stay in Patusan?

Before you read Chapter 8 (*The end of the story*), can you guess what happens? Choose some of these ideas.

1 After a few years Jim returns to England and his family.

2 Jim lives to an honourable old age.

3 He meets a sudden, but honourable death.

4 He is killed by someone he thinks is a friend.

5 He leaves Jewel for another woman.

6 He does something shameful and cowardly.

7 Something happens that destroys the natives' trust in him.

Read Chapter 8, and answer these questions.

1 Why did Captain Brown go to Patusan?

2 What was Kassim's plan?

3 What was Cornelius's advice to Brown, and why?

4 Why did Jim allow Brown and his men to leave Patusan?

5 How and why did Cornelius die?

6 Why did Jim offer himself to Doramin for punishment?

After Reading

1 **Who's who? Match the characters to their descriptions, and then choose the opinion of Jim that best fits that character.**

Marlow	a successful German trader
Stein	one of the young Sultan's uncles
Chester	Cornelius's step-daughter
Rajah Allang	the former trading-post manager
Doramin	a West Australian trader
Jewel	the storyteller
Captain Brown	an old Malay friend of Stein's
Cornelius	an evil seaman

1 'He promised never to leave me, and now he's gone! He's strong, he's fearless, but he's unfaithful!'

2 'I knew he was no good. Once a coward, always a coward! Why didn't he take the job I offered him?'

3 'Did he achieve greatness? I think he did, in the end. Was I right to believe in him? I still don't really know.'

4 'Why did I ever trust the white man? My son is dead because of him. The Tuan has broken his promise to us and he must die!'

5 'How I hate him! He's taken my job and the girl, and now he lives in my house! But I'll get my revenge on him in the end!'

6 'Poor young man! He followed the dream, that's true, but where did it lead him? Such a waste of a life!'

7 'I've got to be careful with Tuan Jim. He could attack me, and then I'd lose everything – my land, money, women, servants . . .'

8 'I'm sure there's some dark secret in his past. Why else would he bury himself in a hole like this?'

2 **Here is a newspaper report about the *Patna*. Put the parts of sentences in the right order, and join them with the linking words, to make a paragraph of five sentences. Start with number 4.**

and / as / by / however / that / when / which

PATNA OFFICERS FOUND GUILTY

1 The *Patna* was sailing across the Indian Ocean to Mecca, with eight hundred passengers on board,

2 _____ fortunately all the passengers were rescued by a French ship.

3 This damaged it so badly

4 At the courthouse today the officers of the *Patna* were found guilty of forgetting their duty,

5 _____ knocked a hole in the metal wall of the ship.

6 _____, the *Patna* did not sink,

7 _____ there were not enough lifeboats for everyone on board,

8 _____ leaving the ship in a moment of danger.

9 _____ the officers were sure the *Patna* would sink.

10 _____ suddenly it hit something in the water,

11 they decided to save their own lives, and escaped in a small rowing-boat.

3 **Jim went to see Stein to discuss the job in Patusan (see page 44). What did they talk about? Complete Jim's side of their conversation.**

STEIN: Well, young man, are you interested in this job?

JIM: _____

STEIN: There's no need to thank me. It's not an easy job I'm offering you. Patusan is a dangerous place, you know.

JIM: _____

STEIN: Of course I trust you. Marlow speaks very highly of you. Now, to business. Here is a letter for Cornelius.

JIM: _____

STEIN: Yes, it is. And he'll be angry with you for taking his job. So be careful of him – and also of Rajah Allang, one of the local leaders, who will probably try to kill you.

JIM: _____

STEIN: You're very confident! However, you may need help.

JIM: _____

STEIN: The best person would be Doramin, one of the Malay chiefs. If you show him this silver ring, he'll help you.

JIM: _____

STEIN: Oh yes, he'll know it – he gave it to me!

JIM: _____

STEIN: Yes, a good friend. We fought side by side in battle. I'm hoping things are all right in Patusan, but I've had no news for over a year. And I hear the river is closed . . .

JIM: _____

STEIN: I'm sure you will, young man. I'm sure you will.

4 **What was the history of Stein's silver ring? Use these notes to describe why the ring passed from one owner to the next.**

1 From Doramin to Stein many years earlier

2 From Stein to Jim before he left for Patusan

3 From Jim to Dain Waris (sent with a message carried by Tamb' Itam)

4 From Dain Waris's dead body, back to Doramin

5 **What were the two messages that Jim never finished? Perhaps the first (see page 71) was to his family, and the second (see page 74) was to Marlow. Complete them with words from the story.**

1 Tell them I am all _____. Tell them I am _____ and well, and doing _____ that I love and can be _____ of. Not a _____ goes by without my _____ about them, but I can never _____ now. My _____ is here, where I am needed, and _____, and respected. Tell them I am happy, if _____ means doing your _____ and making life _____ for other people.

2 An awful thing has happened. Because of my _____, Brown and his men have _____ Dain Waris and several other _____. I am to _____ for this, and I will have to pay the _____. There is no _____ for me. No one can _____ me now. I've had my _____, and my _____ is over. I must now, at once, go to Doramin's _____ and _____ myself to him. It is the _____ of everything.

6 Here are three things that Jim said at different points in the story. Can you explain what he was talking about? Try to use some of these words in your explanations.

conscience, coward, duty, faithful, forgive, guilty, hero,
honour, respect, shame, soul, suffer, trust

1 'Ah! What a chance I missed! My God! What a chance I missed!'

(Jim to Marlow, page 19)

2 'Well, now I know I am all right, anyway.'

(Jim to Marlow, page 51)

3 'If I stayed, I would not be worth having.'

(Jim to Jewel, page 83)

7 Imagine that Jim had time to ask Marlow's advice after Dain Waris's death, in Chapter 8. Here are four possible pieces of advice from Marlow. Which plan do you think Marlow would have advised? Which would *you* have suggested? Why?

1 You're lucky enough to have a woman who loves you. Take her with you, and escape down the river. The villagers won't notice you've gone until it's too late to catch you. You and Jewel can start a new life together in another country . . .

2 You have most of the guns and ammunition in your house. Together, you, Jewel and Tamb' Itam can fight off any attack by the natives. They'll soon realize you are still in control. Stay in your house, and watch out for trouble!

3 You'll have to talk to Doramin, but make sure you have a gun in your hand when you visit him, and get Tamb' Itam to watch your back. Tell the old man you are deeply sorry about his son, but you are not to blame for his death. It was Cornelius who was responsible for the cowardly attack on Dain Waris and his men.

4 Tell Tamb' Itam to collect men and boats at once. Your only chance now is to chase and catch the robbers, then you can bring them back to Patusan, and Doramin can take his revenge on them personally.

8 **Think about or discuss these questions, giving reasons for your opinions.**

1 How can bravery and cowardice be measured? Which of Jim's actions were brave, in your opinion, and which were cowardly?

2 All his life Jim was very conscious of his duty. Which duty do you think should come first?
   - to your country
   - to your family and friends
   - to your own ideas of honour
   - to society's ideas of honour
   - to your boyfriend/girlfriend/husband/wife

ABOUT THE AUTHOR

Joseph Conrad (Teodor Josef Konrad Korzeniowski) was born in 1857, in the Polish Ukraine (then held by Russia). His father's political opinions caused the family to be sent to the north of Russia, where Joseph's mother died in 1864. Four years later his father also died, and Joseph went to live with his uncle.

Conrad had always wanted to go to sea, and at sixteen he joined a French ship and began his life as a sailor, travelling to many wild and dangerous places. In 1886 he received his master's certificate and became a British citizen, and in 1895 he left the sea, married, and settled in England. He had started to write during the long voyages at sea, and he published his first novel in 1895, writing in English, his third language – which he had never heard spoken until he was twenty-one. For the rest of his life he lived quietly in England, until his death in 1924.

Conrad's twenty adventurous years at sea gave him the material for much of his writing – *Heart of Darkness* (1902) was based on his own voyage up the River Congo in Africa. Other famous titles include *Lord Jim* (1900), *Nostromo* (1904), and *The Secret Agent* (1907). Conrad's novels are greatly admired. They are often adventure stories, in which men's characters are tested by danger and difficulty, and they are cleverly told, moving backwards and forwards in time throughout the story.

Lord Jim, which has twice been filmed, is perhaps Conrad's best-known novel. Conrad would not allow himself to have 'favourites' among his novels, but in a foreword to *Lord Jim* he shows his sympathy for Jim's troubled character and his search for his lost honour. Jim, he wrote, was 'one of us'.

OXFORD BOOKWORMS LIBRARY

Classics • Crime & Mystery • Factfiles • Fantasy & Horror
Human Interest • Playscripts • Thriller & Adventure
True Stories • World Stories

The OXFORD BOOKWORMS LIBRARY provides enjoyable reading in English, with a wide range of classic and modern fiction, non-fiction, and plays. It includes original and adapted texts in seven carefully graded language stages, which take learners from beginner to advanced level. An overview is given on the next pages.

All Stage 1 titles are available as audio recordings, as well as over eighty other titles from Starter to Stage 6. All Starters and many titles at Stages 1 to 4 are specially recommended for younger learners. Every Bookworm is illustrated, and Starters and Factfiles have full-colour illustrations.

The OXFORD BOOKWORMS LIBRARY also offers extensive support. Each book contains an introduction to the story, notes about the author, a glossary, and activities. Additional resources include tests and worksheets, and answers for these and for the activities in the books. There is advice on running a class library, using audio recordings, and the many ways of using Oxford Bookworms in reading programmes. Resource materials are available on the website <www.oup.com/bookworms>.

The *Oxford Bookworms Collection* is a series for advanced learners. It consists of volumes of short stories by well-known authors, both classic and modern. Texts are not abridged or adapted in any way, but carefully selected to be accessible to the advanced student.

You can find details and a full list of titles in the *Oxford Bookworms Library Catalogue* and *Oxford English Language Teaching Catalogues*, and on the website <www.oup.com/bookworms>.

THE OXFORD BOOKWORMS LIBRARY
GRADING AND SAMPLE EXTRACTS

STARTER • 250 HEADWORDS

present simple – present continuous – imperative –
can/cannot, must – *going to* (future) – simple gerunds …

Her phone is ringing – but where is it?

Sally gets out of bed and looks in her bag. No phone. She looks under the bed. No phone. Then she looks behind the door. There is her phone. Sally picks up her phone and answers it. *Sally's Phone*

STAGE 1 • 400 HEADWORDS

… past simple – coordination with *and, but, or* –
subordination with *before, after, when, because, so* …

I knew him in Persia. He was a famous builder and I worked with him there. For a time I was his friend, but not for long. When he came to Paris, I came after him – I wanted to watch him. He was a very clever, very dangerous man. *The Phantom of the Opera*

STAGE 2 • 700 HEADWORDS

… present perfect – *will* (future) – *(don't) have to, must not, could* – comparison of adjectives – simple *if* clauses – past continuous – tag questions – *ask/tell* + infinitive …

While I was writing these words in my diary, I decided what to do. I must try to escape. I shall try to get down the wall outside. The window is high above the ground, but I have to try. I shall take some of the gold with me – if I escape, perhaps it will be helpful later. *Dracula*

STAGE 3 • 1000 HEADWORDS

... should, may – present perfect continuous – *used to* – past perfect –
causative – relative clauses – indirect statements ...

Of course, it was most important that no one should see
Colin, Mary, or Dickon entering the secret garden. So Colin
gave orders to the gardeners that they must all keep away
from that part of the garden in future. *The Secret Garden*

STAGE 4 • 1400 HEADWORDS

... past perfect continuous – passive (simple forms) –
would conditional clauses – indirect questions –
relatives with *where/when* – gerunds after prepositions/phrases ...

I was glad. Now Hyde could not show his face to the world
again. If he did, every honest man in London would be proud
to report him to the police. *Dr Jekyll and Mr Hyde*

STAGE 5 • 1800 HEADWORDS

... future continuous – future perfect –
passive (modals, continuous forms) –
would have conditional clauses – modals + perfect infinitive ...

If he had spoken Estella's name, I would have hit him. I was so
angry with him, and so depressed about my future, that I could
not eat the breakfast. Instead I went straight to the old house.
Great Expectations

STAGE 6 • 2500 HEADWORDS

... passive (infinitives, gerunds) – advanced modal meanings –
clauses of concession, condition

When I stepped up to the piano, I was confident. It was as if I
knew that the prodigy side of me really did exist. And when I
started to play, I was so caught up in how lovely I looked that
I didn't worry how I would sound. *The Joy Luck Club*

BOOKWORMS · CLASSICS · STAGE 4

Gulliver's Travels

JONATHAN SWIFT

Retold by Clare West

'Soon I felt something alive moving along my leg and up my body to my face, and when I looked down, I saw a very small human being, only fifteen centimetres tall . . . I was so surprised that I gave a great shout.'

But that is only the first of many surprises which Gulliver has on his travels. He visits a land of giants and a flying island, meets ghosts from the past and horses which talk . . .

BOOKWORMS · THRILLER & ADVENTURE · STAGE 4

The Thirty-Nine Steps

JOHN BUCHAN

Retold by Nick Bullard

'I turned on the light, but there was nobody there. Then I saw something in the corner that made my blood turn cold. Scudder was lying on his back. There was a long knife through his heart, pinning him to the floor.'

Soon Richard Hannay is running for his life across the hills of Scotland. The police are chasing him for a murder he did not do, and another, more dangerous enemy is chasing him as well – the mysterious 'Black Stone'. Who are these people? And why do they want Hannay dead?